Cipher

A Proven Framework to Hire the Best People

Craig della Penna

Third Act Publishers

Book Cover by Megan Petrola

Illustrations by Melissa Thomas-Dubois

1st edition 2026

Contents

Acknowledgements

It is rare that one person working alone can accomplish something magnificent. Whether implicit or explicit, known or unknown, there is usually some source of help or luck that propels the effort. The effort required to create this book is not any different.

Without a doubt, this book would still be resident only in my head and in some spoken words if it weren't for the willingness of Melissa of Third Act Publishers to partner with me on it and bring life to my ideas. Thank you for the kick start, for the creative effort, and for sourcing so many of the wonderful external stories that bring richness to the text. If you are interested in sharing your ideas with the world, you owe it to yourself to give her a call.

Second, Heather and Megan, the two of you are amazing and invaluable partners, and this journey would not only be incomplete but also so much less fun without you on it with me. Whatever the cliché—good to great, leave it better than you found it, pay it forward—call it what you will. Your efforts had a significant impact on this book and continue to have an even more significant impact on me and Aesop, and for that I am deeply grateful.

Thank you to all the clients who gave me inspiration and insight, from the questions you asked to the suggestions and critiques that you provided. Not only in this book, but as we evolved traditional scorecards into more meaningful Ciphers® as we worked together on live projects... that's where the true development occurred.

Thank you to the Aesop team. Rather than demanding a rest during the break between hectic projects, you engaged. Whether creating the resources, designing the website, editing a draft (yet again) or simply tolerating another "great idea", you've been with me every step of the way. We couldn't succeed without us, and "u" are a critical part of "us". Thank you deeply and from my heart.

Finally, an acknowledgement is not complete without acknowledging the most important people in my life. Caroline, Lucy, Finn, and even Sherlock the Wonder Poodle...none of this matters without your love, support, and devotion. Thank you for bringing me my greatest joys and teaching me my most important lessons - I love you all.

About the Author

Craig della Penna is the creator of the HireBest® system and founder of Aesop Partners, LLC. He has spent the past 25 years advising business leaders at leading Fortune 100 companies, private equity-backed middle-market companies, and family-owned businesses on issues of talent and strategy.

Over time, his focus has evolved from financial guidance to strategic and operational guidance and finally to talent—the focus of his life for the last fifteen years. His passion lies in helping wildly successful business leaders create even more success for themselves.

His experience includes:

- 250+ satisfied clients.
- 2000+ structured interviews conducted.
- 170+ organizations diligenced.
- 800+ leaders trained.

He discovered that the number one way to create more valuable companies is by improving the quality of the people that managers hire and put on their teams. The HireBest system has given him a 90% success rate in identifying top talent. Now, he is proud to share the knowledge he has used to generate that success with you so you too can build the right teams around you, starting with the most important element: the Cipher.

This is the origin of HireBest—a desire to move beyond advising on senior-level roles one-by-one and instead to help business leaders at all levels make better hiring decisions. Sharing these tips is our way of helping to truly democratize talent.

Finally, his most significant accomplishment and responsibility is being a devoted husband and father. When he is not helping leaders build high-performance teams and companies, you can find him on the high seas with his wife, two children, and his ferocious standard poodle Sherlock.

Introduction

Whenever I talk to team leaders with a top-tier track record of hiring exceptional talent, I find a key consistency to their approach: they bring the same seriousness to hiring as they do to the rest of their business. They think through what they want in the role, set a strategy to define it, and treat the selection method as a critical decision process. In short, what makes them great at hiring is that they follow a Cipher-driven process, whether they call it that or not.

The Cipher is the structured output that results from thinking through what the hiring manager needs in the role. This process brings a clear focus to the specific Outcome this role must achieve and therefore the most important Deliverables required to get there.

The Cipher document becomes a roadmap for identifying the right person to hire, getting them up to speed during the onboarding process, reviewing annual goals, and even for performance coaching. In short, it is the critical foundation for creating stronger teams and management processes.

This book is designed to both teach you the lessons that have made a dramatic difference in my own hiring outcomes and also to be a practical guide you can use as you create a Cipher for yourself. I suspect that you'll come back to the book over time, digging into those areas you may have skimmed through the first time and gaining even more value from reading it.

In Part I, I provide all the reasons why you should love the Cipher as much as our team does! I share my experience gleaned from hundreds of clients who have made hiring mistakes and what those mistakes cost the company and the manager. I then present specifics on everything you can potentially gain from using a Cipher.

Part II teaches you how to actually make a Cipher. I'll take you step-by-step as you learn the key components of a Cipher and how to build it for your role. For now, you only need to know two things:

- A Cipher is a structured and prioritized method of zeroing in on what matters most for a specific role.
- It differs from (and complements, not replaces) a job description. The job description is fine as a recruiting/advertising document, but the Cipher is the hiring selection document.

In Part III, you will work through how to strengthen and improve your Cipher. This includes involving others to gain their input as well as running through a handful of simple checks to make sure what you've built can properly support you in making the best hiring decision. Think of this section as the graduate-level course for the basics you learned in Part II.

In Part IV, you are done creating! Now is the time to put your Cipher to use. We'll discuss grading it as well as reinforce the importance of mitigating decision biases, covering the 9 most common biases a Cipher helps to avoid. I'll also share tips on how to use a Cipher as part of onboarding your new employees and beyond.

Finally, in Part V, I will wrap up my final thoughts and discuss how you can apply the thought process behind the Cipher to other key decisions in your life.

Learning is good, knowing is great, and doing is best

This book is designed to guide your skill development, *not* to be a theoretical lecture! Tackle each chapter, work through the "Read it, think it, do it" exercises at the end of each chapter, and start practicing. Bounce ideas off others and jot down their thoughts. Don't just read, but be thoughtful. When the book asks you a question, visualize someone (like me) asking you the question.

Your hard work will gather momentum once you have taken the first few steps toward changing your approach. The more steps you take, the more you will find yourself armed with an innovative approach *that works,* and you'll be on your way to building outstanding teams.

Want to take your learning to the next level? Access additional resources at www.hirebest.ai!

You'll see this icon whenever there is a specific online reference available. Some are free, some have a modest premium, but all are thoughtfully designed to help you excel at this craft!

Above all, I want you to be successful on this journey *and* to love the process of getting there! I also hope you learn more than just how to use the Cipher. I've interspersed little bits of leadership lessons I've learned from doing over 2,000 executive interviews on the front lines of human capital consultancy, having made all the mistakes and lived to tell the tale.

The origins of the Cipher

I am a data nerd. I created my first spreadsheet on Lotus 1-2-3, and I still remember some of my old "/fs" commands. I was the teaching assistant for the Decision Sciences course in my MBA program, known as a mouse-free keyboard warrior, and make a spreadsheet almost whenever I encounter a complex decision.

From this analytical foundation, I made the oh-so-natural move into squishy people topics! I learned about the scorecards and competency lists that are key to the Topgrading approach (thank you, Brad Smart!), and saw how much better they made the hiring process. But I also saw my clients struggle to build them themselves, and too often found them turning into a better organized version of the job descriptions they sought to rise above.

Once I realized that there was a proven way to assess talent and saw the benefits it provided to my clients, I got frustrated. While I could help to ensure that the top leader was the right match for the company, I didn't have the scale to help all leaders within a company hire the right talent. Holding onto this secret that could be used to support the whole company felt radically unfair!

As a result, I formalized the HireBest approach to make it accessible to hiring managers everywhere. The Cipher is the cornerstone of that system. People are complex, yes, but they are also analyzable. The experiences and skills they bring can vary, and figuring out whether to hire Person A or Person B can often seem daunting.

But by breaking a role down into its parts and measuring a person's fit against those parts, you will make a better decision. In fact, the combination of creating Ciphers to define the roles plus using a structured interview process has, for me and for others, driven a 90%+ success rate when hiring and predicting how people will perform in their new roles.

Across the thousands of interviews my colleagues and I have conducted over the last decade, when I give someone a thumbs up, it is likely that, a year later, that person is still delivering results. Most hiring managers struggle to achieve a 50% hit rate, and most unstructured interview approaches average around 25% accuracy.

Managers just like you have seen dramatic improvements in their hiring abilities by applying a Cipher-driven method. HR and talent acquisition veterans with decades of experience tell me how the HireBest system has upended their entire approach, and they experience far better results based on their new skills.

The HireBest complete system has four primary components, but the Cipher is the key to it all:

- Developing a Cipher to know what you're looking for,
- Using a structured interview approach that eliminates bias,

- Engaging master techniques to unlock the stories and experiences that help you evaluate fit, and
- Finalizing the decision through a data-rich process and utilizing better reference techniques.

This book will teach you the first of the four components to get you immediately on your way to better hiring practices!

If you want to hire and build your team in a predictable, reliable, and measurable way, keep reading and working through the exercises in this book. Not only will you get to learn the concepts and build a Cipher specific to your needs, but you will unlock the ideas and strategies that will take you to that next level of performance you hunger for.

So, if you're ready to follow my lead and radically change the nature of your team, let's go! It's a great privilege to share what I know with you. I hope my experience both informs your learning and inspires you to grow and improve your own leadership.

« PART I: A Reality Check »

The definition of insanity is doing the same thing over and over and expecting different results.

Albert Einstein, theoretical physicist

CHAPTER ONE

Gaining Conviction

The Old Way Just Doesn't Work

Do you have the perfect team? This would be a team that has all the skills you need to achieve your goals, that work effectively with one another, and provide you with all the leverage you need so that you can focus on the highest value activities that you alone are best positioned to do personally. And if you have that team, are you confident that if you had to add someone to the team or backfill an unexpected vacancy, you could do so with at least 75% certainty of hiring the right person?

If you and your managers can answer yes to these questions, congrats! Consider yourself truly in the top 1% of business leaders, put down this book, and go start shopping for your next new yacht or supercar or vacation home! Everyone else, keep reading!

The reality is most managers cannot answer yes to those questions because most managers have not had the opportunity to learn the art and science of hiring the best talent. Most managers have either never received great training on how to hire their team or the "traditional" interview training they received seemed to make sense but never quite delivered. That's why so many new hires fail.

I have been hiring for years. Isn't what I am doing good enough?

Probably not. According to a study by Leadership IQ, 46% of newly hired employees will fail within 18 months, while only 19% will succeed in their role.[1] The old tried and true hiring techniques deliver results worse than simply flipping a coin. If you wouldn't flip a coin to choose a candidate, why would you use an approach that produces similar results?

When explaining our services as a consulting firm, our biggest competitor is resistance to change. Most people have false confidence that what they do is good enough, or lack faith that hiring is a muscle that they can improve. They've tried other interviewing courses, they've tried using search firms, and nothing ever really made a difference. And most people have never added up the true cost of hiring the wrong person, instead simply accepting it as a cost of doing business.

Hiring mistakes cost you time, money, and aggravation!

When hiring managers make a mistake, it costs the company approximately *15x the candidate's salary* for the average mid-to-senior level role.

Of course, the damage varies slightly depending on the level in the organization—a little lower if you go down to the entry-level and as much as 25x for CEOs. Everyone pays attention to the obvious dollar costs (salaries, recruiting fees, moving expenses, etc.), but the highest costs are the hardest to see.

For example, consider the cost of hiring the wrong sales leader for an enterprise software business. This individual needs to sell $1 million in annual revenue plus oversee a team of six, who should generate an additional $4 million in revenue. Further, let's assume that the company takes action quickly, exiting this person in nine months (more often I see this stretching on for a year or more). We'll assume a $150,000 base salary for this role.

What's the cost about $125,000 or so, right ?

Nope. Hard dollars lost in the signing bonus, relocation costs, separation costs, recruiter fees, and salary paid for the person who did not add value equals about 1.5x salary or $225,000.

Their boss and peers lost productivity from their roles as they tried to help them get up to speed, impacting their value contribution by about 0.5x to 1.5x of the individual's salary.

As a result of the individual's poor leadership, they missed their quota, and their team did as well. With a 25% team shortfall to quota, that's $1.25 million or 8x the leader's salary. For a non-sales role, ask yourself what business damage the wrong decisions can have on the bottom line, whether missing opportunities that your competitors seize or making bad choices that hurt your standing in the market. It's not hard to recall some blatantly bad decisions companies have made over the years, and imagine how many millions of dollars the company would have gladly paid to avoid those losses. But I'm too much of a gentleman to list them all here!

The new leader hired two people who (un) surprisingly didn't work out either. But the underperforming leader gave them solid performance reviews, and it will take some time to work them out of the organization. Meanwhile, one of your top-performing reps decides this is all too much, and they'd rather work for your competitor. At $100,000 each for the two underperformers, the combination of hard dollar costs, productivity, value shortfalls, and the morale impact of the lost high performer easily equates to another 5x the leader's salary.

You can see how quickly a full accounting of losses reaches 15X and can go even higher for C-suite roles![2] A quick internet search will turn up a long list of CEOs who did massive amounts of harm to the companies they led—far more than the 15x salary outlined above.

Now, multiply the losses accumulated through just one mis-hire across your entire organization and see how hiring becomes a multi-million-dollar responsibility.

Think about a recent hiring mistake you or your team has made. How much time, money, and frustration did that cost you?

If you have yet to experience that, consider this from a future perspective. What will it cost the company if they get the next hire wrong?

Use this table and cost averages to come up with the total number so you can see how much money a Cipher-driven approach can save you.

Cipher Savings Worksheet	hirebest	
Salary, signing bonus, relocation, separation costs, and recruiter fees.	1.5 x base salary =	
The distraction caused to the boss and peers trying to get the new employee up to speed.	.5 x base salary =	
Missed market opportunities and leadership failures.	8 x base salary =	
Errors in hires that a mis-hire made affecting performance, loss of other team members, and poor morale.	5 x base salary =	
	Total impact =	

Three common failures drive the vast majority of hiring mistakes

We have found three major areas where the traditional hiring process fails to deliver:

1. The role is not defined well enough to source and evaluate candidates

I repeatedly hear, "I guess I don't know what we are hiring for. We just need a sales leader who can sell and get the team selling too!"

How will you find the right person if you don't know what you're looking for? Worse yet, how will you communicate your goals to that great candidate you just met?

M.P. McEnrue conducted a study of 340 California mid-level managers and found that the job performance of employees is a joint function of competence *and* role clarity. Her work also showed that the job performance of more competent employees is more strongly affected by role ambiguity than that of their less competent counterparts![3]

Not only will a Cipher-driven process improve your hiring batting average, but the clarity it provides helps strong new hires be even better!

2. Managers try to go it alone

Peers, bosses, and other stakeholders can provide alternative perspectives that add depth and precision to the hiring process. Even when the manager is a subject matter expert on the technical aspects of the role, and has the interpersonal fit required to succeed, they might miss key components that need to be included in the Cipher. Somewhat related, we've seen many hiring processes fall apart when the hiring manager thinks they've reached the finish line but their boss had a completely different view. Cipher development specifically includes others because different stakeholders expect different things from the role.

When expectations are aligned, the new employee will have a much better likelihood of delivering success in the role.

3. Interviewers use an unstructured interview approach

An unstructured interview is when the questions vary depending on who is asking them, or which candidate they're seeing, and overall, it's a nice friendly conversation... with no clear objective. The most common example is the classic resume walk-through, asking the candidate to essentially repeat what is already on paper, hoping secretly they can use some useful tidbit to make a decision. This approach is easy but also results in the *statistically proven worst results possible.* If you are in an interview that feels more like a conversation, and find yourself talking about your kids, hobbies or sports teams, chances are you've found yourself in one of these.

There are hundreds of studies that offer convincing evidence of using structured interviews versus unstructured interviews. In fact, there are so many industrial and organizational psychology studies on the topic that you can also find numerous meta-analyses synthesizing all the studies into another study itself! If you're interested in the topic, the reference below is quite strong.[4]

In the end, traditional approaches do not collect the data needed to measure someone's performance objectively against a framework for what has to be done in the role. The team at Aesop Partners regularly achieves that 90% success rate in hiring that was mentioned earlier! Having an accurate Cipher is the cornerstone of that process and why I wrote this book.

Key chapter takeaways

- Hiring mistakes cost time and money. Period.
- Three points of failure consistently keep managers from hiring their best teams, and the Cipher plays a role in eliminating all of them.

Read it, think it, do it

Note: Each chapter will end with a short exercise to help you bring the ideas presented to life for you personally. Complete them to help you become a master of hiring great people.

One of the leading causes of hiring mistakes is the misalignment of expectations.

Looking back at your own hiring record, or as an employee taking a new job, what benefits would you have gained by having a clear and succinct understanding of the expectations in the role:

Chapter Two

Six Benefits of a Cipher-Driven Approach

If you're motivated by avoiding a loss, then Chapter One was for you! You learned about the pain that you will avoid by following a Cipher-based process.

For those who are more motivated by achieving gains, then this is your chapter. I am going to outline all the benefits you'll achieve in addition to avoiding a loss.

When you use the Cipher as the basis of your hiring process, you will:

1. Save time and money

Using a Cipher-driven approach will reduce hiring errors, saving significant time and money. But Ciphers also offers savings within the hiring process itself. Knowing what you need at the beginning of the search helps you refine your hiring process to screen out candidates who are obviously not a good match.

On average, a corporate job posting receives 250 resumes.[5]

Do you have the time to sift through 250 resumes only to find a handful of maybes? Or to meet countless candidates as you try to "get a feel" for whether someone is a good fit? In the long list of a job description, the specificity of priorities gets lost in the noise of wish list requirements and often non-meaningful proxies like "years of experience" or certain degrees. A Cipher lets you (or others) screen efficiently for specific, relevant accomplishments. You end up with fewer resumes to read while improving hiring success rates.

2. Create alignment across the hiring team

It's incredible how often people *think* they agree on the details of any given role but do not.

The Cipher process ensures alignment, starting with a comprehensive yet short description of the role that sticks in your brain during interviews. This becomes the shorthand all team members use to reinforce what matters in the role.

An iCIMS study showed that 80% of recruiters believe they have a good or very good understanding of what a manager is looking for in a role.[6] At the same time, 61% of hiring managers believe that recruiters have a low-to-moderate understanding. That doesn't sound like alignment to me!

This failure to communicate is what the Cipher process solves. Once both sides of the house specify the role in a way that creates clarity and alignment, the hiring process accelerates as recruiters can better target exactly what the role truly requires.

3. Shorten the onboarding and training process

Rather than starting a new job and spending the first 90 days reconciling the priorities of their boss, their boss's boss, and peers, new hires have a meaningful document that lays out what matters most in their new role. They can come out of the gate running with the Deliverables, including critical metrics and milestones, outlined in the Cipher. A lengthy job description cannot get someone to the same level of clarity and prioritization in the same timeframe.

4. Reduce the time needed to coach up underperformers

Addressing poor performance requires a lot of work when you don't have role clarity. Documenting, gathering facts, having tough conversations, spending untold hours coaching, and monitoring performance all add up. Many of those wasted hours are often spent arguing with the employee, trying to convince them that what you're asking for really is a part of their job.

The clarity of the Cipher, including delineation of the cultural requirements needed to succeed at the company, creates a success roadmap for the underperforming employee to follow. Now it becomes a simple question of whether they are executing on the requirements they were originally measured against. In situations where you still might need to conduct performance coaching, the Cipher makes it easier with its specific expectations.

5. Build a scalable process rather than relying on luck

Too many hiring processes rely on a manager "just knowing" what good looks like in the role. Implementing a Cipher-based approach gives you a system for aligning on the key requirements of a role, tapping into the expertise of those around you.

Then, you can evaluate candidates in a systematic, quantitative, and strategic manner. It is also a learnable skill that your team can adopt themselves, increasing their hiring batting average without having to always rely on you for the final say.

6. Close the candidate you really want

Savvy applicants are drawn to the clarity that a Cipher-based process provides. Candidates often reject a job offer because they didn't like what they saw in the hiring process—such as seeing company leaders who are not on the same page and instances where interviewers outright contradicted each other about the opportunity.[7]

High-quality candidates usually have an average job search time of only ten days.[8]

If you approach hiring with an "I'll know it when I see it" mindset, you'll lose the best candidates to competitors who know what they want.

Doing the work upfront will give you the conviction to move fast when you finally find that star.

Bonus! You'll strengthen your data-backed decision-making muscles.

At the end of the day, a Cipher-driven mindset is about taking a structured approach to the *how* of decision-making rather than simply defaulting to habit.

Once you adopt this mindset for hiring, you can apply it to make other life decisions so much easier. This includes buying a house or a car, choosing the right dog breed, or even marriage, as you'll discover in the closing chapter.

Craig's real-world story

A client was experiencing massive growth and needed to increase headcount by more than 30% within a year. After four months, they were behind, and they needed to hire 1,200 people over the fiscal year! This included frontline sales reps, customer service agents, software engineers, marketers, etc.

Hiring managers traditionally wasted too much time interviewing unsuitable candidates. They had started using the Cipher for their C-suite recruiting but hadn't implemented the change throughout the company, leaving most of the hiring to happen the old way: grab the last job description, tweak it, get the posting out there, and start interviewing. Talent Acquisition did its best, but managers were left shooting in the dark.

We launched a highly accelerated rollout of the HireBest training system to all of its hiring managers.

Seven months later, they met their hiring goals by conducting fewer interviews for each new hire because the recruiters and hiring managers knew exactly what they were looking for. A year later, first-year attrition had halved, indicating that they were hiring people who were a better fit for their roles.

Aesop's modern fable

Using data in recruiting and hiring has become increasingly crucial for businesses. A few years back, JetBlue teamed up with academics at the Wharton School to look at new ways they could leverage data analytics to predict employee fit and performance.[9]

Ryan Dullaghan, JetBlue's Director of People Data Insights, shared details at the Wharton People Analytics Conference in 2015. The company used a flight attendant profile for hiring that included a set of eight key characteristics, the number one being how "nice" these employees would likely be toward demanding customers.

Alongside Wharton, they discovered customers (or passengers) strongly preferred helpful employees over just "nice" ones. Being helpful balances out the negative effect of someone who is not that pleasant. The JetBlue team revised its flight attendant profile to better identify top candidates as they sift through the 125,000 applications they receive each year.

They can quickly eliminate noise with the right profile (or Cipher) to staff up and positively impact the bottom line. Their new approach resulted in higher employee engagement, a rise in retention, and a 12% decrease in total absences—all important in reducing flight delays. On the customer side, JetBlue gained a half-point in its Net Promoter Score (NPS). The lesson: a data-driven approach creates results.

Key chapter takeaways

- A Cipher is about discovering what you truly need in a role. Once you have that clarity, you can adjust your hiring methods to fill positions faster by focusing on candidates who are the right fit.
- Using Ciphers ultimately results in spending a lot less wasted time in both hiring and managing your team.

Read it, think it, do it

The Cipher will help reinforce a data-backed approach to decision making for hiring. But that mindset can be applied throughout both your professional and personal life.

Where else would you benefit from adding more structure and data around your key decisions:

« PART II: Building a Cipher »

Leadership and learning are indispensable to each other.

John F. Kennedy, 35th President of the United States

Chapter Three

The Cipher Decoded

At the heart of a Cipher is the four-letter acronym *CODE,* which will help you remember the four key elements of a Cipher. By following this formalized, prescriptive process, you ensure you close the candidate you *need*, not the candidate you think you want.

Sometimes to truly understand a new concept, it's helpful to see a picture of it as well as to contrast it against common knowledge. Let's explore the detailed differences between a Cipher and a job description.

The most serious mistakes are not being made as a result of wrong answers. The truly dangerous thing is asking the wrong question.

Peter Drucker, management consultant and author

Job Cipher vs. job description

We previously offered that the Cipher differs hugely from a job description—let's break that down.

The Cipher is a succinct document that explicitly lays out, in a prioritized fashion, how success will need to be achieved in the role you're looking to fill. It creates a clear understanding of what the person will need to do to be successful in the role, how "integration into our existing culture" is defined within the organization, and what is required to manage their team.

Ultimately, this framework establishes uniform comparison across multiple candidates for any role, enabling better decision-making based on data rather than a gut feeling.

In a few pages, you will see an example of a Cipher followed by a job description for the same role. Note that for brevity, only the first two Deliverables have Efforts. While this is an obviously simplified example for an Ice Cream Shop Clerk, the usability and clarity jump right off the page.

In just one document, you know exactly what success looks like and how it will be achieved in five simple Deliverables. And, who knew there was more to this job than just being friendly and scooping ice cream?!

Then contrast that with the job description. It summarizes the role responsibilities and requirements of the job for potential candidates, but without any prioritization nor any of the internal information necessary to specify how success will actually be achieved. It includes job specifics like location, schedule, travel, education, and pay. Some of these things are legally required to be explained, so that's an important aspect to complete.

Overall, we value the job description for what they are good for, which is to inform external candidates about the role —we just don't think they're useful for evaluating candidates. Yet the job description is often the only document outlining the role. As a result, it's what people use for most hiring decisions, causing managers to struggle with accurately rating candidates.

Obviously it is far easier to evaluate a candidate against the Cipher versus the long laundry list of specifications in the job description.

Skeptical? Match your job description with your annual goals. Once they stop laughing, most people acknowledge that their job description lacks the precision to drive behavior like goals do (or a Cipher does).

Ice Cream Shop Clerk Cipher 
Charge: A friendly window clerk to grow profitable repeat business for a popular ice cream store.
Outcome: Maintain $250 average hourly sales while delighting customers, growing by 5% annually. **Outcome Clarification:** Delighting customers is based on: • Maintaining a historical average of one unsolicited compliment card weekly. • Supervisor/manager informal review of customer interactions. • Maintaining weekly customer volume numbers.
Deliverable: Solicit ice cream orders in a friendly and timely manner. **Efforts:** • Smile when greeting customers. • Say hello and apologize for delays if you cannot serve them within one minute of arrival. • Stick to the script: "Welcome to the Ice Cream Shop. How may I delight you today?"
Deliverable: Suggest additional options for the customers to try. **Efforts:** • Suggest sprinkles if the customer does not ask for them. • Suggest waffle and dipped cones, maintaining our 20% average. • Offer the special flavor of the week, providing sampling to 20 people per shift.
Deliverable: Deliver the appropriate amount of ice cream/product the customer ordered.
Deliverable: Maintain an accurate cash drawer.
Deliverable: Live the Ice Cream Shop culture.

Ice Cream Shop Clerk Job Description

The Ice Cream Shop, a specialty ice cream and novelty store with locations throughout the metropolitan area, is seeking applications from qualified candidates for employment as team members in our stores.

Required Skills

- Fluency in English with excellent written and oral communication skills
- Experience working with the public/a diverse group of customers
- Excellent interpersonal skills
- Strong organizational abilities
- Ability to work well independently as well as in a team environment
- Flexible schedule, including nights and weekends
- Ability to learn quickly and pay attention to details
- Desire to meet or exceed sales goals
- Able to maintain the highest levels of customer service
- Working knowledge of cash drawers and order systems
- Previous sales and/or marketing experience and demonstrated success are a plus
- Previous experience increasing customer engagement and loyalty a plus

Required Experience

- Must have a high school degree or higher
- Being currently enrolled in an accredited college or university program or bachelor's degree in a related discipline is a plus

Preferred Experience

- Experience working in the food service industry or customer service field
- Experience working with the public and consumers
- Managing teams or other workers a plus

Job responsibilities include:

- Greeting customers
- Taking orders and fulfilling them accurately
- Maintain the cash drawer and submit it at the end of shift
- Communicate with team members about the operations of the store
- Attend staff meetings as needed
- Stand for extended periods of time, if not most of, each day
- Move/access supplies such as ice cream buckets and toppings up to 25 pounds
- The noise level in the work environment is moderate to noisy
- As needed, work a flex time schedule to meet customer needs during peak times
- Any other duties that maybe required by staff or as deemed necessary
- Answer the phone as needed

Compensation includes a base salary. Part-time employees are NOT eligible for vacation, health insurance and retirement 401(k)

Specificity matters

There needs to be a mechanism that enables a clear choice, linked to the specifics of the Outcome you want to achieve. That's where the Cipher comes in.

It's a little like asking someone who the best musician is: Drake, Elvis Presley, or Taylor Swift?

The correct answer is all of them; it simply depends on your criteria!

(As of this publication date, Drake has the most certified units sold of an individual musician worldwide,[10] *Elvis is the best-selling solo artist based on pure album sales,*[11] *and Taylor Swift is the highest grossing live music artist.*[12]*)*

Now, translate that into a business setting; determining the best of anything requires even more specificity.

Consider a sales representative. In one company, the best consumer software sales reps must be able to close low-ticket prospects quickly and move on to the next sale.

In a B2B enterprise software company, the best reps will design a calling strategy to get into a prospect company, network to the people who matter most, develop a detailed set of requirements, and engage in a months-long solution-selling effort.

But if you ask your recruiter to find a sales rep, and they give you the best, which one will you end up with? I don't know and without a Cipher, you don't know either.

Building specificity helps you make the right data-driven choice and determine the best candidate for the job. As you create the Cipher, remember that this is an internal document. It ensures internal alignment regarding what you are hiring for and what you need this person to do. Therefore, be candid and include specific growth projections or other descriptors to create an accurate Cipher.

Tailor or create a new Cipher for every distinct role

Can't I just use my last Cipher for this role? The short answer is no. First of all, if you are hiring a replacement for anything less than the best employee you've ever had in that role, I strongly suggest you make a new Cipher or at least critically question the last one you used.

Don't assume the lack of success the last person had in the role was 100% driven by the employee alone. Consider that your process may be partly at fault. Perhaps you did a near-perfect job of hiring someone for your Cipher, but there was a critical element missing from that Cipher.

A Cipher is uniquely created for a specific role. Most people understand that the Cipher for one functional leader, like the Head of Accounting, will be dramatically different from one needed for the Head of Sales. But even within a department, a Cipher that works for one manager may need to be at least heavily tailored if not completely redrafted for a different manager in that same department. The Cipher needs to reflect what that department, and that manager, need that person to do in order to succeed... and that can change from manager to manager.

The question comes down to:

If two different managers would rate the same employee in the same exact manner and expect the same output with the same exact culture fit, then yes, use the same Cipher.

If not, you will benefit the most by thoughtfully tailoring your existing Cipher or, ideally, creating a customized document from scratch.

Given the realities of psychological biases, I strongly recommend building a bespoke Cipher rather than tweaking an existing document. Most people resist making major changes to an established product, taking a shortcut by using what they already have on file. After six months, they usually recognize their mistake of hiring someone who is an ideal fit for the Cipher they borrowed from someone else, but not a great fit for what they actually needed.

Learn the *CODE*

CODE is the heart of the Cipher and will help you remember the four key elements of a Cipher. Whether you use the template in this book or scribble it on a cocktail napkin, the *CODE* will get you there!

C is for Charge, the short phrase that captures the essence of the role.

O is for Outcome, the primary way you will measure success in the role.

D is for Deliverables, the five to seven most important steps to achieve the Outcome.

E is for Efforts, how the Deliverables are achieved.

The following example shows the first page of a Cipher for a Director of Sales with the Charge, Outcome, Deliverables, and Effort completed. Upcoming chapters will go in-depth into each part of the CODE and provide detailed steps to help you become an expert at building effective Ciphers.

Director of Sales
Cipher

hirebest

Charge: A scrappy Director of Sales-Northwest to re-energize the sales force and institute process rigor for a fast-growing company.

Outcome: Grow revenue from $20-35 million in three years in our core business plus $5 million from new products.
Outcome Clarification :

- Revenue is product revenue, not service revenue.
- Core business is XYZ device sales.
- Contribute to new product development in support of product growth.

Deliverable: Directly train, mentor, and ensure quality of sales approaches throughout the territory.
Efforts:

- Directly manage the Seattle office sales force. Provide coaching and training both in the office and via ride-alongs. As needed, do the same with the other four offices.
- Identify best practices across the region and ensure they are applied across the territory, especially in low-performing offices.
- Develop relationships with physician and non-physician KOLs. Invite reps into those relationships to help them grow and learn.
- Conduct quality training on sales skills and evaluate to ensure successful learning and adoption of new practices.
- Boost engagement scores and decrease turnover. Rep turnover is currently 27% in the northwest compared to the company average of 15%.

Craig's real-world story

It is crucial to design the Cipher for what you *need* over what you *want*, and to do this *before* you are influenced by candidates in the pipeline (even subconsciously). Several years back, I had a client hiring a new CEO for their organization. The prior CEO was a deeply beloved, charismatic founder who relied on gut instincts more often than process and data. Using the job description, the hiring team met with various candidates, and by the time I was engaged to help, they were down to two finalists. That's when we began building out the Cipher for this specific role.

The company's board was leaning toward an ex-military candidate who brought considerable company experience; they believed he could help instill the focus on process they needed. As a result, subconsciously more so than consciously, they created a Cipher reflecting the need for a hard-charging, brass-knuckled leader who would not be easily dissuaded from the mission. The mandate outlined a leader who would instill process, upgrade standards across the organization, and drive a loose federation of individual divisions into a cohesive unit that marched in sync. Not surprisingly, their preferred candidate performed exceptionally well against this Cipher and was hired.

Approximately 12 to 18 months later, the company found that its new CEO was implementing too much bureaucracy and process into its formerly entrepreneurial company. Furthermore, this decisive and convicted leader didn't like his views questioned by the board and would not ask for help. Needless to say, this was not the CEO the company really needed.

So what went wrong? The process went sideways when everyone became enamored by the first candidate. They had such a clear view of what they thought they would get if they hired the first candidate that it biased their view of what they really needed.

Although they tried to be objective in their creation of the Cipher, they were subconsciously creating a framework that reflected what they liked about Candidate A. Ironically, by the time they were parting ways with Candidate A almost 18 months later, Candidate B had sold his company, making him available once again, and they hired him.

Had the Cipher been developed from scratch before meeting either candidate, I'm sure the second candidate would have won out the first time, saving the client millions of dollars in company value (and about 18 months) as they struggled to gain traction towards their goals.

Aesop's modern fable

Billy Beane of "Moneyball" fame inherited one of the smallest budgets for any MLB team player salaries in 2002.[13] Frustrated with his inability to outbid other teams for talented players, he took a different approach. He called Paul DePodesta, a Harvard alum and professional sports executive interested in data analysis.

They combed through decades of data on hundreds of individual players to devise a better strategy for recruiting players. They discovered scouts were overlooking statistics that could better predict a player's performance vs. relying on subjective things like attitude or whom they had played for in the past. In short, scouts were asking the wrong questions to assess talent. The scouting process failed to include individual components that made up a player's performance and match that to what the baseball team needed—much like hiring managers looking at academic qualifications or years of experience as a proxy for the responsibilities the individual needs to take on in a new role.

In the end, Beane's big bet on analytics paid off. Despite having a smaller budget, the Oakland A's won against bigger teams and made history by winning 20 consecutive games in American League baseball. Recruitment in sports was transformed as Beane's method made player assessment a quantifiable process rather than a subjective one. Analytics always trumps a gut feeling.

Key chapter takeaways

- A Cipher, with its specificity and concise nature, consistently outperforms a job description.
- The four key elements of the Cipher can be recalled quickly with the acronym CODE.
- Like Billy Beane, the Cipher helps you find candidates who excel at the specific and meaningful parts of the role (Deliverables) so they can push the team to success (Outcomes).

Read it, think it, do it

Pull out the job description for your own role. How well does that reflect what you actually do?

What's missing?

What unnecessary fluff is on it?

How many of the qualifications do you fall short of?

You shouldn't be surprised if you fail against half the qualifications! Know that this says more about the effectiveness of job descriptions at predicting success than about your being successful in the role.

Chapter Four

C for Charge

The Charge reflects the essence of the role and establishes a shared language for prioritizing the job's key aspects for everyone involved in the hiring process.

Charge

Title
+
Style Adjective
+
Change you seek
+
State or growth phase of company

Charge:

The qualitative and pithy statement capturing the essence of the role.

Sitting at the top of the Cipher, this one-sentence header outlines succinctly the impact you want this individual to have on the company. If you have to expand to two sentences to capture your thoughts, you are not describing it concisely enough.

Articulating what you want and need

Imagine yourself at a barbecue and it turns out your neighbor is the best search professional in the world. It's like LinkedIn and Korn Ferry got married, and this person was the offspring of their union.

While chatting, she asks, "How are things going at work? Every time I see you, you look exhausted!" You explain to her that you have been doing your job, plus the work of a critical vacant position, *and* recruiting for that open position. It dawns on you that you have been given a perfect opportunity to get advice from the best of the best.

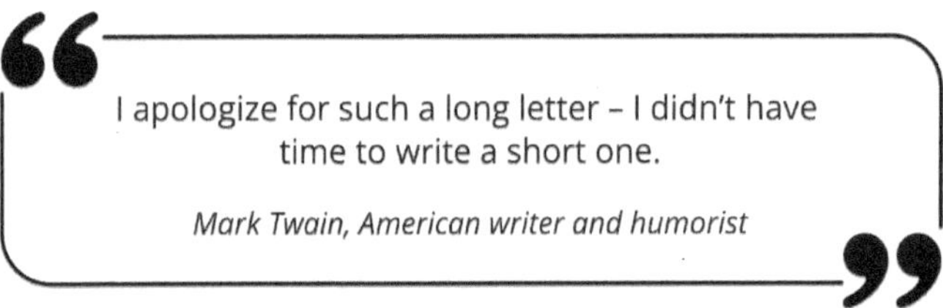

You tell her, "I'm looking for a top-notch sales director who will boost the company's revenue." She offers some thoughts, but you leave the conversation a little deflated—she didn't seem to understand what you needed. In this situation, not laying out the specifics of your goal resulted in a dead end.

You need specificity, even more than you think is necessary

No one can do it all. You need support to find the proverbial needle in a haystack.

A method of communicating the crux of the role internally and externally is what you need so that everyone, even you, can keep what is most important in the job top of mind.

Distill the Charge down to as short a statement as possible. It will be the phrase you constantly repeat and playback to ensure everyone stays centered on what matters most. This is critical, so be prepared to spend 15 minutes or more creating this one sentence!

There are four key elements of the Charge:

1. The title

Though it sounds basic, getting the title right is vital. Within companies, there is often an internal understanding of what a director vs. manager vs. vice president entails.

Select an internal title that immediately conveys the role's position within the company's hierarchy to the interviewing cohort. Then, consider how you will advertise the role and whether that specific title can or should be used so that the interviewing team knows how to refer to the position during the interview.

Use specific terms that people outside the company can understand.

Think about the type of person you want to attract and whether they would be interested based on the title. If you have the budget and need for an HR Director, don't call it a Divisional CHRO. Why waste everyone's time sorting through the resumes of applicants seeking mid-six-figure compensation packages when your budget has a $100,000 maximum? If you're an energetic, market-disrupting start-up, what's a fresh take on the title that would work for you and attract the type of person that would fit well with your culture?

Remember that while you won't share the Cipher publicly, you will use the title with candidates. Ensure you note in the Cipher how the role is advertised externally so the interview team references a consistent title to the candidate.

2. The style adjective

The style adjective describes the most important interpersonal trait you're looking for in a new team member. Regardless of the required work, this flags the "how" of their working style.

Use one or two adjectives *at most*. You have too many descriptors if you need to use an Oxford comma.

What is this role's non-negotiable, job-relevant, yet unique attribute? For example, if everyone in your company is typically fun and outgoing, that might not be the characteristic you highlight since your interviewing team will look for that naturally. Instead, what else is critical for this role?

Use adjectives that are colorful, descriptive, *and* meaningful. The goal is to give other interviewers a clear sense of what they should listen for and probe into during their time with the candidate.

For example, let's say your new hire must possess a unique critical thinking ability to anticipate potential challenges. Some might say the candidate should be smart. Different people interpret *smart* in different ways; e.g., book-smart vs. street-smart, educated vs. quick to learn, or simply thoughtful and inquisitive.

Instead of using a generic adjective like *smart*, consider the actions that this person will drive and use descriptors such as strategic, forward-thinking, anticipatory, dynamic, or planful.

3. The change you seek

Think about your business or department: how will it be different as a result of filling this role? This is your opportunity to define this person's impact at the highest level. If you had to cost-justify this position, why would you invest their salary and associated expenses right now? Is it to overhaul the department? To launch a new service? To upgrade a rickety technology infrastructure? To drive a substantial increase in customer satisfaction?

What challenges are causing you to hire for this role right now? How do you bottom-line that need?

Use a more aspirational statement vs. a technical measurement. How will filling this role contribute to the organization's overarching strategy?

In the Outcome statement, which you will build in the next chapter, you will be able to define success more measurably.

In an HR department, potential "change you seek" elements could be something like implementing top-notch people processes and development tools or turning around the coarse culture in our factory.

Use language that speaks to the essence of what they will be doing. Are they building something from scratch? Are they improving upon a predefined model? Do they need to halt one activity and turn the organization in a completely new direction? Or are they simply increasing the capacity of the function to handle more volume? Each of these scenarios speaks to very different skill sets. Spelling that out informs the hiring team.

4. The state or growth phase of the company

The Charge structure's last leg provides context to inform the rest of the Cipher accurately. For example, if the change you seek is to *launch a new product*, how that gets done at Procter & Gamble is different from Joe's Organic Body Wash, so the essence of the role will differ as a result.

What is significant about the company's or our department's growth phase that will define the right person for the role? The drivers behind a person who thrives in a steady-state vs. a startup vs. turnaround situation vary greatly.

As with the other elements above, use language that evokes a clear and meaningful picture. *Continuing growth* is weak compared to *above-market growth,* and better yet, it would be *a company that will double revenue in X years.*

Now, let's return to our conversation with our friend, the recruiter. Rather than saying something like, "I need a Sales Director who is, umm, good at selling," you now know to use the Charge: "I need a [scrappy] [Director of Sales] to [re-energize the sales force and institute process rigor] for a [fast-growing company]."

Simple does not mean watered-down

The four-part formula for the Charge provides the foundation on which you will build your Cipher. As with many things, while simple in form, do not underestimate its power.

There is a difference between a meaninglessly simple explanation and a richly concise understanding of a complex topic. Often, in business, people add additional complexity in an attempt to increase the usefulness of an idea. Complexity and utility are opposing forces at work and must be balanced.

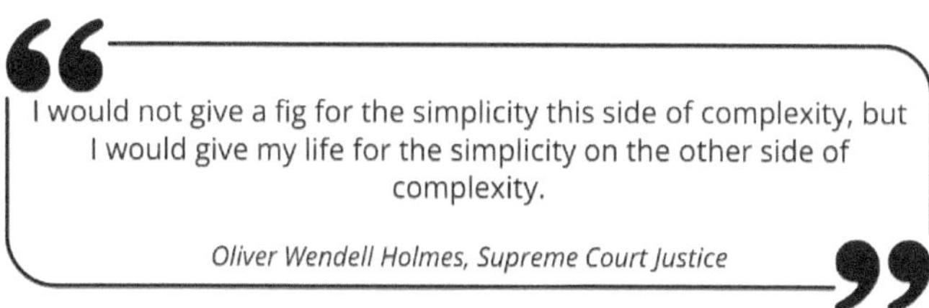

Take the time to reflect carefully on your word choices. The result must be accurate to you and clear to others taking part in the hiring process. The 10 to 15 minutes you spend developing the Charge will save you untold hours and frustration from a lack of alignment with the rest of your colleagues.

Upload an existing job description to our GenAI Cipher generator to see suggested style adjectives for your role.

Craig's real-world story

A client was looking to hire a general manager for a business unit, which was struggling to hit their performance goals.

The hiring manager knew that to drive success with this business unit, the new GM would need to challenge many legacy conventions to deliver on the new strategy.

As they described the innovative and disruptive leader they were looking for, we put that specific language into the Charge and played that back to the team. They did not like what they saw. The reality was that while they wanted the energy and vision of a fresh perspective, once they saw it on paper, they realized that a truly "disruptive" leader would be detrimental to the ongoing success of other business units.

Working through the process of getting agreement on specific descriptors helped them realize they were looking for more of an *evolution* than a *revolution.*

Aesop's modern fable

NASA launched the Mars Climate Orbiter in 1998 to study Mars, spending $125 million on a 338-kilogram robot. Heralded as a crucial space exploration step, it would act as the communications relay for the Mars Polar Lander.

Instead of celebrating the next exploration phase, the Orbiter's teams were shocked to watch their work go up in flames. In September 1999, after almost ten months of traveling to Mars, the Orbiter burned up in the atmosphere, breaking into pieces.

The post-mortem discovered that the navigation team at the Jet Propulsion Laboratory used the metric system in their calculations. At the same time, Lockheed Martin in Denver calculated data in inches, feet, and pounds.[14] This detail, which was supposed to be embedded into both company's rigorous quality control procedures, was not discovered even during the nine months it took the spacecraft to make its 461-million-mile flight to Mars. Both teams failed to confirm some of the basic assumptions to ensure they used the same language for their work.

Key chapter takeaways

- Crafting a dynamic and explicit Charge includes using four key elements:
    - Title
    - Style adjective
    - Change you seek
    - Growth phase of the company
- The devil is in the details *and* the translation. Getting the Charge right is the first and critical step in ensuring everyone on the team knows exactly what success looks like for the role.
- Keep it simple. Be brief *and* be clear by keeping the Charge focused on what absolutely matters the most.

Read it, think it, do it

Begin crafting a Cipher specific to you and your organization by creating the Charge on the worksheet below. It can be for a position you are actively recruiting for, or you can use your job for this exercise.

Cipher Charge Worksheet	**hirebest**
Title • What is commonly used in your company? How can you tweak it specifically to the role's true purpose? • How will the title attract the person you want during recruiting?	
Style adjective • Use only one or two powerful adjectives. • What personality trait or characteristic encompasses how this person drives success?	
Change you seek • What is the impact that defines success in the role? • Does this change tie into the growth strategy of the company? • Is the phrase aspirational in nature?	
Growth phase of the company • Be specific and creative. Some examples include turnaround, fast-growing, steady growth, and M&A focused.	
Now, put it all together in one sentence: **The Charge**	

Chapter Five

O for Outcome

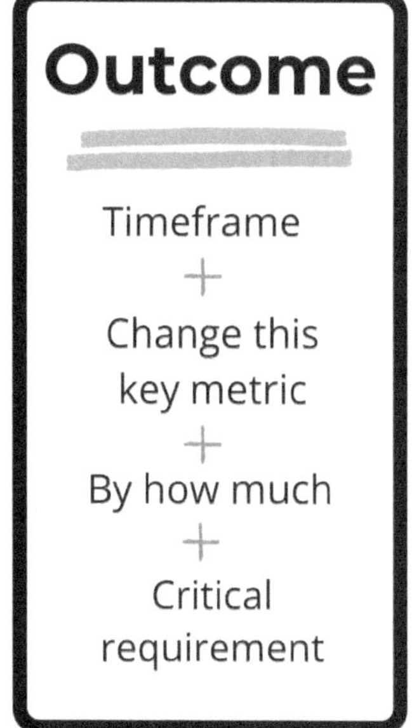

The second component of the Cipher is the Outcome. While the Charge outlined the essence of the role and the change you want this individual to create, the Outcome brings specificity to that change.

Outcome:

The positive impact you want this individual to have on the company.

Specifically, and measurably, once this individual has succeeded, what will be different in the company because of hiring this person? What tangible result will you be able to point to as proof that you hired the right individual, and that they got the job done?

The four parts of the Outcome

There are four key elements within an Outcome statement. The exact order isn't critical, but all four must be included to enable an as objective measurement as possible for your specific role.

Returning to our example from Chapter 4, the "old you" at the BBQ may have quantified the sales goal as "at least more than last year...10-20% per year." If the description stopped there, that would give our friend, the recruiter, little to go on. She needs more direction to find someone with relevant experience.

Luckily, you now have a new Outcome formula to guide you toward a more productive conversation!

1. Timeframe

The timeframe for results is captured within the Outcome as the starting point. You want to set a specific end date by which you expect the Outcome to be achieved. For most roles, I recommend using a two- to-three-year interval.

We have found that interviews are far less effective at predicting future behavior beyond roughly three years as the person changes and the role changes.

However, if you only think about what you need next year, you are likely specifying only part of what you really need and not thinking about the bigger picture i.e., clients often focus on the need to fix a specific shortcoming that is causing pain today but the real hiring need goes beyond simply patching a hole and will be with you for much longer. So, spell out that plan.

2. Key metric to be changed

This is the specific and most important item to be improved as a result of their success in the role. By the end of the above-mentioned timeframe, how will you precisely measure and conclude that they did a fantastic job? For sales roles, revenue will often be the critical metric; for others, it can be a different indicator, such as lead generation, digital engagement, customer satisfaction, or other KPIs.

By definition, one must be able to measure or otherwise objectively rate a key metric.

The metric also needs to focus on what is most important to the organization's or department's overall performance. Key metrics should tie back to the company's overall strategic objectives. For example, for a mid-level marketer, you could count the number of newsletter sign-ups or form completions online, but are those actions the true measure of success? Or is it qualified leads, sales appointments, consumer market awareness, etc?

Some roles will fit the model easily, as they have specific financial targets or quotas to achieve that naturally become the Outcome. Other roles will have an Outcome that is harder to define because they are less quantitative. You must ensure that it is objective and measurable in some way, even if it is not quantitatively defined.

For example, I have worked with clients who believe their most important Outcome for an HR Business Partner is reducing attrition. Other clients have said improving employee engagement across the department is the core of the position. Still, others want to increase the percentage of senior roles with "ready now" successors as the core to the company's push toward growth.

One of those Outcomes is not better than another, but each client had a specific reason for hiring a new HR Business Partner, correlating to a specific Outcome. The key is to identify what is most important in *your* role and make sure you have a way of measuring performance. The only wrong Outcome is the one that *is not* aligned with what you need!

Upload an existing job description to our GenAI Cipher generator and we'll propose a draft Outcome for you!

3. By how much—defining the goal for improvement

Once you have defined your metric, the next question is defining the scope of change. For example, this might be a particular revenue number, such as growing sales of $2 million over 12 months. Adding additional information, such as increasing from $2 million to $4 million, is an important criterion that allows you to better measure a candidate's fit for the role. Even better would be the percentage of growth required, such as taking channel sales from an annual run rate of 5% to 10% a year. Ultimately what is the expected level of improvement you need to see in the key metric in order to determine that this new hire has been a success?

4. Other critical requirements (relative to that metric)

This fourth element is technically optional, but I use it about 80% of the time when creating an Outcome. As "the key metric to be changed" is *the most important* element, sometimes there are secondary considerations that need to be thought of as well. Sure, you may want sales to double over a specific timeframe, but it may be equally important that a portion of that growth comes specifically from new products. Or that while they double revenue, they need to at least maintain current margins if not grow them. This is where you can specify that tradeoff.

Are you looking to expand in one new geographic area while keeping the rest of the business stable?

Does the person need to not only grow sales but specifically also add a number of new customers each year?

This is the place where you can add any unspoken rules that may significantly impact how success is achieved.

Now that you understand the four components of the Outcome formula, let's look at it in action in our Director of Sales example. With a clearer outcome statement, you now have several specific elements that you can use to screen new candidates against. Specifically, as you consider a pile of resumes, do the candidates have any stated evidence of their ability to perform a similar role in a similar situation?

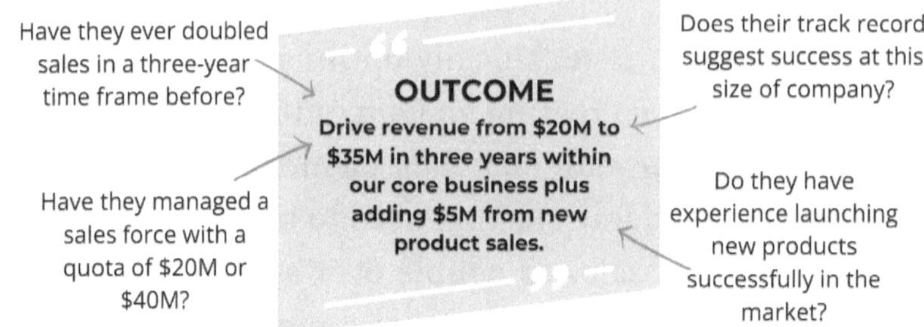

Outcome clarification statements

Ideally, the Outcome you create will be a single sentence that successfully covers the positive impact this person will have on the organization. However, sometimes, that isn't enough to provide the other members of your hiring team with enough of an understanding of what success really looks like in this role.

This is especially relevant in less quantifiable roles. It's also necessary where there is any specific jargon in the Outcome statement that needs a greater explanation for the broader set of stakeholders using the Cipher.

You can add a couple more bullets in the Outcome section of your Cipher to provide clarification. For instance, with our example above, you added the clarification that the revenue needed to come from product, not service, sales and that the "core" is "xyz device sales." These were added to address questions that the interview team may have. However, I urge you to resist the temptation to add more solely because you have room--less is truly more!

Craig's real-world story

Our client was looking for a Vice President of Software Engineering to focus on application development. Their Outcome was, roughly paraphrased, "Launch four internal applications or major upgrade releases over the next 18 months using agile methodology."

Their outcome clarification bullet points specified the need to:

- Implement an agile culture across the department,
- Focus on a roadmap of critical maintenance items and infrastructure needs
- Better represent Engineering in critical leadership meetings.

In this case, the outcome clarification went far beyond clarifying the Outcome statement to become a full set of Deliverables. The hiring team struggled to screen candidates and narrow the pool down to a group of finalists. It was nearly impossible to reach consensus on who to invite back to a second round of interviews because each team member prioritized a different piece of the Outcome and based on the "clarification." Once the misalignment was identified, they revised the Outcome to prioritize application development and found a successful leader.

Aesop's modern fable

Failing to understand the interconnectivity of the four elements of the Outcome proved to be the downfall of People's Express, the airline that grew almost overnight in the 1980s. When the government deregulated the industry, the company aggressively trained its people to be the best.

Don Burr, the founder, had an unwavering vision to grow the business "as big as possible" without regard to scalability or understanding the havoc such a non-specific mandate could cause.[15]

The CEO's vision was for highly engaged workers to act like owners, taking on any task in their purview to create "the best" airline.

They deprioritized specific expertise in favor of a generalist model, while also dramatically changing their business model. They went from a low frills airline to offering premium service, from contractors to their own employees for growing operations, etc.

The combination of a lack of specificity in role clarity (e.g., what an Outcome statement is designed to support) coupled with a rapidly changing strategy was too much.

Creating a company that is "as big as possible" and "the best" by having employees take on whatever job was needed is fundamentally not scalable nor designed for success.

The workforce burned out with rising rates of health issues and divorce amongst employees and leadership. Rather than adjust the expected Outcome for his leadership team, Burr pushed everyone to the brink.

The company declared bankruptcy, and Texas Air purchased it in 1986.

Key chapter takeaways

- If you don't know where you're going, you will probably never get there...other than through sheer luck. Clarifying the definition of success in the role, as objectively as possible, is a critical part of making the best hiring decision. The Outcome statement defines the success that this role, and the company, will achieve when you have hired the right person.
- There are four distinct parts of the Outcome:
    - Timeframe
    - Key metric to be changed
    - "By how much" the metric will change
    - Other critical requirements
- Outcome clarification statements can be added to provide necessary color and descriptive language that the single sentence cannot provide.

Read it, think it, do it

Create your Outcome for the Cipher you are working on using the four key elements outlined in the worksheet.

Cipher Outcome Worksheet	hirebest
Timeframe • Two to three years is the best practice.	
Key metric to be changed • Objectively measured. • Ties into the company's overarching strategy.	
By how much will that metric change • Be explicit.	
Critical requirements • Create caveats or specifics like "X while also doing Y."	
Now, put it all together in one sentence: **The Outcome**	

Chapter Six

D for Deliverables

With the Charge and Outcome completed, you have identified the essence of the role and clarified the benefit the organization will gain from this new employee.

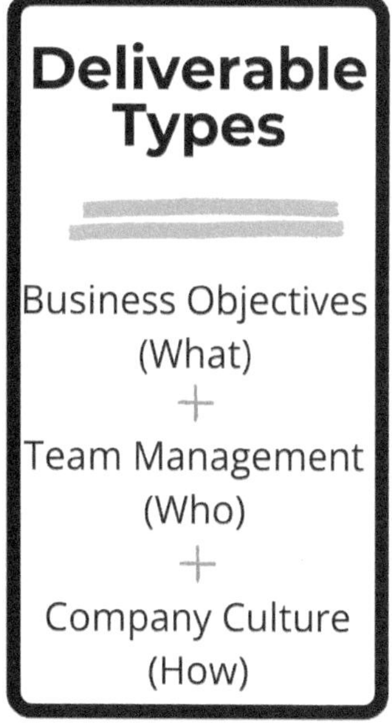

The next step is to outline the Deliverables, which describe *how* the individual will achieve the Outcome.

Deliverables:

The set of five to seven accountabilities most critical to achieving success in the role.

In the simplest terms, these are the prioritized set of five to seven accountabilities most critical to achieving the Outcome.

They are not and should not be the comprehensive laundry list of everything a person could do in the role.

Timeframe and number of Deliverables

The Deliverables are how the employee will achieve the Outcome you want; essentially, you're breaking down your Outcome and Charge into more precise components with greater granularity. You may look at our definition of Deliverables and wonder, "What's so special about five to seven accountabilities?" It's not as random as you might think. Instead, this is our conclusion after years of testing in the field.

You cannot hope to predict success across an extensive range of accountabilities within any interview process. An interviewer's mind cannot hold it all in during the interview, and the process to get enough data on all of those deliverables would be overwhelming. Bluntly, assessing a candidate on too large a list of deliverables can lead to false precision. It might make you comfortable when you hire but will not serve you well with any level of accuracy.

This limitation also forces prioritization of what is *critical* to achieving the Outcome. Prioritization enables a more effective interview and creates alignment across the hiring team about what the role *really* needs to do. This will be discussed later in the Cipher Strengthening and Rigor Testing chapters. In my experience, I have found that five to seven deliverables encompasses the most salient components that drive the highest level of value.

Finally, it's important not to forget the timeframe you created during the Outcome. I hope you followed our guidance and generally use a two- to three-year time horizon for the Outcome; remember, that is the timeframe of peak predictability. But ultimately whatever you choose, it's important to make sure that your Deliverables are matched to what is needed (and possible) in your Outcome timing.

Whatever timeframe you use, it must be consistent across the Charge, Outcome, and Deliverables.

The three Deliverable types

Deliverables comprise three types: Business Objectives, Team Management, and Company Culture. These are the *What, Who, and How* of getting stuff done.

1. The What (Business Objectives)

These are what most people think of when they hear Deliverables. These are the specific accountabilities and tactical objectives that must be accomplished to arrive at the Outcome.

2. The Who (Team Management)

The specific requirements for managing a team. If you are hiring an individual contributor, you can disregard this. But if the person you're hiring will have a team underneath them, this is one of your most critical Deliverables.

3. The How (Company Culture)

This refers to the specific traits and actions needed for a new person to do well in your company or department based on your distinct values and customs.

The nuances of each Deliverable type

The What: Business Objectives

"Business Objective" Deliverables will make up most of your Cipher and address the tactical aspects of what must be accomplished to achieve the lion's share of the Outcome. With a typical limit of five to seven Deliverables, this means that most Ciphers will have four to five "Business Objective" Deliverables, leaving one for the Culture and one for Team Management.

Let's return to the Director of Sales Cipher as an example. Combining our Charge and Outcome. The hiring manager is looking for a scrappy director of sales who can double revenue from $20-40 million, with $35 million coming from sales in core products and $5 million from new products...but *how* will they do this?

Let's say the hiring manager recognizes one of the current problems is how the sales representatives each make up their own sales approaches and execute them reasonably inconsistently. The new sales director must bring order to the chaos. Therefore, our number one Deliverable is to "Directly train, mentor, and ensure the quality of sales approaches throughout the territory."

Unaided data is the best data! When building your Cipher, start with a blank sheet of paper and sketch out the Business Objectives and other Deliverables before looking at job descriptions or additional guidance.

Continuing with our Director of Sales example, the full list of Deliverables follow below:

- Directly train, mentor, and ensure the quality of sales approaches throughout the territory.
- Professionally manage a tenured and customer-centric team, implementing more accountability.
- Develop new strategies to increase the size of our market.
- Partner with Operations to build account management and implementation capabilities.
- Be an influential member of the Northwest leadership team and develop partnerships with key peers.
- Integrate as a part of our existing culture.

Note that Deliverable #2 is the Team Management Deliverable, and Deliverable #6 is the Culture Deliverable, which will be discussed later.

Looking across the six Deliverables, can you envision the type of individual who might be successful in this role vs. someone who might not?

Having created and read hundreds, if not thousands, of these documents, I see the need for a strong manager who can innovate to grow the business while systematically maximizing the existing business. That's quite different from a rainmaker who will open up new accounts, which is still very different from many other variants of a sales director role.

As you work to create your own Business Objective Deliverables, use the following questions to get started:

- How will they achieve the Outcome? If the new person was at your desk right now, and you needed to give them direction on how to spend the next week, what is the most important thing they should do? If your answer is highly detailed, (e.g., make 25 phone calls to prospects), then summarize it at a higher level (e.g., generate new leads leading to new customers). If high level, great—that's a deliverable and we'll add more specificity in the Effort section next.

- What are the "results" produced in the role today (or needed from this role, if new), and how best do you summarize that activity (e.g., produce financial reporting, generate new business, develop a new product, increase market share)?

- What other major initiatives do they need to drive or oversee?

- What are you most unhappy about what the current incumbent isn't doing or isn't doing in the way you'd like it to be done?

- Related to that, will they inherit something they need to keep going well, rebuild something entirely broken, or start something from scratch? Consider this from the overall role perspective and for specific components, such as systems or reporting.

- How much do you need them to follow a plan vs. devise a plan vs. create a new strategy? How strategic do they need to be? Is being forward-looking, analytical, or market-focused necessary for success?

- What level of customer focus or other interpersonal interactions are required in the role? What is the expected engagement with stakeholders and what type of personality traits are needed for success?

- Does the individual need specific domain experience? What is crucial for the right candidate to excel at coming into the job or be able to come up to speed quickly? (Be careful here... lazy job descriptions rely heavily on "must have X years of experience" as a cop-out for really thinking about what they actually need to be able to do.)

Finally, as you create the Business Objective Deliverables, either rank order or re-sort them according to priority as you go. Where the Team Management and Company Culture Deliverables fit into their sections is described further below.

See how our GenAI Cipher generator can help you create Deliverables!

The Who: Team Deliverable

There is no question about it; if you are hiring someone who will supervise others, then you will need to create a Team Management Deliverable. Furthermore, in almost every situation, you should prioritize this as your first or second Deliverable. The reason why is simple: the role of a manager is to accomplish work through their team, especially as they become more senior in the organization's hierarchy. Managers and leaders produce more through their teams and less through their actions as they progress up the corporate ladder.

While all Ciphers for a managerial role must have a Team Management Deliverable, the specifics of that Deliverable can vary significantly based on the team's needs. A Fortune 500 CEO inheriting a high-performing executive team requires a different Deliverable than a first-level manager in an underperforming region of the same company. Ultimately the greatest success is achieved by framing most Team Management Deliverables into one of five types below:

The Five Most Common Team Management Deliverables

1. Build and lead a new team
2. Manage and maintain a high-performing team
3. Strengthen and develop an existing team
4. Improve a currently underperforming team
5. Integrate and/or unify multiple teams

Maybe one of those team scenarios perfectly reflects your situation. If not, write a new one or pick the one that feels closest to your circumstance and return to it after the next chapter (Efforts). You may find crafting a great Deliverable headline easier once you have thought through and developed the detailed Efforts.

The How: Company Culture

Every Cipher needs to incorporate a cultural element. There are too many hiring mistakes made where the candidate had the right technical abilities or tactical experience but could not integrate into the specific culture of the company or department.

At the same time, culture is about more than just whether someone has a good or bad attitude. Culture is how the organization operates, what behaviors it places the highest value on, what it will and will not tolerate, and fundamentally how the work gets done day-to-day.

Defining your culture with clarity and objectivity is crucial. This is not the time to be aspirational about *what you would like* the culture to be but to be honest about the traits and behaviors that make someone successful within your company.

The most important aspect of the Culture Deliverable is to put a line in the sand regarding the role you want this person to play within your ecosystem. You'll define the specifics of what that culture is within the Efforts. Similar to the Team Management Deliverable, consider whether one of these five Deliverables appropriately matches your situation:

The Five Most Common Company Culture Deliverables

1. Integrate as a part of the existing culture
2. Be a change agent within the culture
3. Help unify multiple legacy cultures
4. Help build culture as part of the team
5. Define and roll out a new culture

Clarifying Deliverables, especially Company Culture, reduces bias in your hiring process

Clarifying all the Deliverables, but especially the Culture Deliverable, is where the Cipher and the supporting HireBest interview methodology can drive meaningful bias-reduction benefits. At its core, HireBest is about specifying the data you need to find in an interview, having a standardized process that is common to all candidates, and evaluating that interview data in a consistent manner. This goes far to mitigate any interviewer bias that may cause overly positive (or negative) interview results found in low quality "unstructured" interviews.

Specific to Culture, people often see "culture fit" as someone who thinks and acts similarly to the group. The problem with that approach is its impact on opportunities for people who aren't highly similar to those making the decisions. Additionally, the organization can lose out on extraordinary talent because of an underdeveloped or unsophisticated cultural fit assessment.

There is a massive benefit to individuals, companies, and society at large if hiring managers take the time to define culture in meaningful, accurate, and bias-free descriptions of how the work actually gets done rather than the ultimately incorrect proxies that make everyone feel comfortable.

In short, thoughtfully defining what constitutes culture fit in your organization is a critical step in your Cipher creation and a worthy use of time. If not, you risk interpreting "fit" largely as a measure of how much a candidate is similar to the interviewer.

Be blatantly honest about what your culture is really like vs. an aspirational picture of what you want the culture to be. A person's ability to work in the manner required by the company, i.e. culture fit, is a leading factor in people succeeding or failing in new roles.

Enlist others when defining your Culture Deliverables and Efforts

We'll talk about engaging other stakeholders in the Cipher Strengthening chapter more broadly but know that requesting help is especially valuable when expertise exists that you might not possess.

The best place to start when defining the culture is with your HR department. In a perfect world, they will have a way of describing the culture that is not only objective and accurate but also helps to ensure consistency. Even if they do not have an off-the-shelf definition, partnering with them to create a Culture Deliverable pays off in at least two ways.

- First, their expertise can help avoid illegal or discriminatory elements while emphasizing objective and selectable behaviors.
- Second, Culture Deliverables should not vary wildly across a company. While there may be differences in engineering and sales cultures, most companies have a consistent overall culture.

While culture is vital to determining someone's success in a role, typically place this at the bottom of Ciphers. This does not mean it's the least important! Rather, listing it at the bottom is a way to prevent it from being lost "in the middle" and instead to keep it top of mind.

Guided by rules, not scripted by formula

Unlike the Charge and Outcome, Deliverables don't fit into a neat and compact formula.

Each role is different, and there can't be a formula for every situation since this is a book, and not a supercomputer. Instead, consider the three Deliverable Rules as a pathway to follow in creating the right Deliverables for your position.

Deliverable Rules

Be specific and clear

\+

Show understanding without minutiae

\+

Be mutually exclusive

1. Be specific and clear

The more specific and clear you are, the easier it is to select against the Deliverable and the higher the likelihood you hire successfully for the role. Read the Deliverable again later—do you still understand what you meant when you wrote it?

2. Define the role without getting bogged down in minutiae

The statement should not be a monstrous, run-on sentence with three conjunctions, nor so short as to have no meaning. "Implement a new system" can be misunderstood as it lacks details regarding what system, whether it is a system selection / purchase or simply programming, or whether you are starting from scratch vs. having to convert from the old one, etc.? The Deliverable has to be something an interviewer can use to know what data to listen and probe for during an interview.

However, the descriptors need to be concise enough that a person can quickly see what is important. A more effective Deliverable would be "Evaluate options and install new ERP system replacement with Manufacturing management capabilities." The more specific *and* straightforward you can make the Deliverable, the better your Cipher will be.

3. Assure mutual exclusivity

You only have five to seven Deliverables to work with, so use them well. Each Deliverable should be a self-contained unit representing a distinct aspect of the role, separate from any of the other Deliverables. The experience "muscles" required to succeed in one Deliverable should be distinct from what is required in the others. I.e., if by proving they can do one certain activity, a candidate can score highly on multiple Deliverables, then you are at risk for over-rating that element and underestimating the other factors that go into this role.

Taking the example above, it would be wildly redundant in most cases to have one Deliverable for the ERP implementation and another for the WMS. Don't try to split out the ERP component of the system from the WMS component; the underlying technical expertise and interpersonal characteristics to achieve either of those are so similar that splitting them into two is a waste of a Deliverable. You will probably grade both of those the same anyway, so keep them together.

Don't forget that your total number must also include the Company Culture and Team Management Deliverables (if applicable). Therefore, challenge yourself to force prioritization (and eliminate non-priority accountabilities) rather than jam them all in and create all-encompassing mega-Deliverables.

Craig's real-world story

You need to get the five to seven Deliverables right, but you *also* need to understand their relative importance.

One Aesop Partners client struggled with this concept specifically. They were looking to hire a new division manager for a struggling region. Retaining customers has been a challenge for everyone in the role thus far. Their top Cipher Deliverable was "Grow our market share with existing customers and meet their other service-related needs." Hiding near the bottom was "Oversee implementation of the corporate operational improvement plan."

All agreed that "Jon" was a perfect hiring candidate despite his lack of operational expertise. Ultimately, they hired him since he was only lacking in the least prioritized Deliverable.

Six months later, Jon quit after failing to turn around the division's performance. He and his boss agreed that the real issue was the operational problems across the branches that were impacting customer service, and therefore retention. Jon's exceptional sales abilities, as impressive as they were, could not fix the real roadblock to growth.

Aesop's modern fable

Elon Musk, the vocal CEO of Tesla, promised in the summer of 2018 that Tesla would make 10,000 Model 3 sedans a week — and then delivered about half of that.[16]

During an interview with Gayle King shortly after the June 2018 shareholder meeting,[17] Musk took responsibility for the delay and missed targets. He conceded he pushed the team to do too much at once, installing too much new technology into the Model 3 simultaneously rather than in stages. He failed to understand the sophisticated factory technology. Ultimately, they built an automated system that slowed down production rather than sped it up.

He said his highly optimistic nature got the better of him, and he recognized he needed to be more accurate in forecasting the future. To be sure, Musk excels as a visionary, but, in this case, he missed the details needed to make the dream a reality.

Key chapter takeaways

- Prioritization is key. Your goal with the Deliverables is to define the most important elements, NOT list out all of them.
- There are three types of Deliverables:
    - The What: Business Objectives
    - The Who: Team Deliverables
    - The How: Culture
- While challenging the first time, rigorously and authentically defining what it takes to succeed in your company's culture will lead to much better hiring outcomes, and, reduce interviewer bias.

Read it, think it, do it

Draft the five to seven Deliverables for the Cipher you are creating. Considering the questions and prompts in this chapter, write down everything needed to achieve the Outcome.

With a clear mind and your brainstorming complete, refine that list into a concise set of the top-level Deliverables for the role.

Double-check your work:

- Have you captured the most valuable actions the current or prior individual in this role took to drive value?
- Have you included what isn't getting done right now that is needed from the next person in this role?
- Is each Deliverable specific and clear? Could someone understand it immediately?
- Is the Deliverable statement concise without too much fluff that detracts from the intent?
- Does each Deliverable stand on its own as being mutually exclusive?
- Can the Deliverables be achieved in the time allotted in your Outcome?

Cipher Deliverable Worksheet	hirebest
Business Objectives • The What	1. 2. 3. 4. 5.
Team Management • The Who • Mandatory if they are a manager	6.
Company Culture • The How • Mandatory for all	7.

Chapter Seven

E for Efforts

We close out our four *CODE* chapters with E for Efforts. Efforts will describe how each Deliverable will be achieved.

If the Deliverables are the topic sentence of a paragraph, the Efforts are the supporting statements that complete the story.

Efforts:

The unique, role-focused ways the Deliverables will be accomplished.

Efforts outline specific actions and behaviors needed to complete the Deliverable successfully. They also can include more specificity behind the Deliverable where necessary. You may have a Deliverable like "Manage our outside contractors to deliver marketing collateral," and the Efforts can specify "Manage 8 to 10 independent contractors and three agencies."

Just as you prioritized your Deliverables down to the top five to seven, Efforts also need to be prioritized generally to three to five per Deliverable. Remember that prioritization of what is *most critical* is essential to creating a Cipher and running an effective interview. You cannot possibly remember all the potential "nice to haves" during an interview, nor collect adequate data against all of that, and thus need to focus only on what is most important.

The three guiding principles of Efforts

1. Define how success is measured

Ensure that your Efforts clearly outline the definition of success for the Deliverable. Let's consider an accounting clerk. One of their top Deliverables is to "Provide accurate daily and monthly financial statements." Ideally, the perfect clerk will *never* make mistakes herself and *always* catch everyone else's errors before our Controller ever sees them.

But *never* and *always* aren't realistic, so what is a more achievable definition of success? One way would be to consider the impact on others, namely her manager. A better Effort would be to "Maintain less than 1% unresolved daily variances and have fully proved balances within five days of month-end."

2. Specify the most critical details

As mentioned above, there is an art to including the most critical details without including all the minutia! Making assumptions about what you can generally assume people will be able to do and what is most critical to success will help you find the right balance.

Back to the clerk example, your Efforts do not need to include an understanding of basic math. You may want to specify "Independently prepare trial balances" or "Conduct preliminary analysis when ledgers are out of balance." Yes, basic math is required, but you don't need to bog down the Cipher to spell out that level of minutia. Once you have enough data to prove that your candidate can prepare trial balances and analyze discrepancies, you can assume basic math.

At the same time, consider any specific technical skills that the person must possess for the Deliverable that aren't obvious. For example, it may be logical to assume that an accounting clerk knows basic Microsoft Office programs. However, if fluency in a specific bookkeeping package or analytical software is a non-negotiable requirement, include that in the Efforts along with other qualifications. But be sure to only include those "mission critical" technical requirements; if you would rule out someone for a lack of expertise there, include it. If it's a nice to have, don't bog down the interview (and role) with less important minutia.

3. Identify what is unique about this role at this company

As you consider each Deliverable, one way to determine the *most critical* efforts to include is to consider how the role at your company differs from the average expectation of the role. For example, the unique aspect for the clerk illustration is the somewhat older technology that the company uses. Information is stored in cumbersome databases and requires intermediate programming skills to retrieve data efficiently. Yet the clerk needs to retrieve that data to complete work daily. Therefore, the manager is not just looking for someone with basic accounting skills but also who is technologically proficient enough to overcome this obstacle. The hiring manager might consider adding something like "Extract data from Great Plains via SQL database queries in an AS400 mainframe environment."

Building out the Efforts in our example

As a last step in understanding the Efforts of a Deliverable, let's return to the Director of Sales Cipher (below). You will see how the five Efforts listed for the Deliverable cover the most important components of achieving success, including defining what success looks like. The first Deliverable is to "Directly train, mentor, and ensure the quality of sales approaches..." In order to do that, the individual will need to identify sales best practices, provide direct/classroom training and coaching, lead the way through crucial relationship development and handover, and boost knowledge scores as proof of their success.

Putting it all together:

Director of Sales
Cipher

Charge : A scrappy Director of Sales-Northwest to re-energize the sales force and institute process rigor for a fast-growing company.

Outcome : Grow revenue from $20-35 million in three years in our core business plus $5 million from new products.
Outcome Clarification :

- Revenue is product revenue, not service revenue.
- Core business is XYZ device sales.
- Contribute to new product development in support of product growth.

Deliverable : Directly train, mentor, and ensure quality of sales approaches throughout the territory.
Efforts :

- Directly manage the Seattle office sales force. Provide coaching and training both in the office and via ride-alongs. As needed, do the same with the other four offices.
- Identify best practices across the region and ensure they are applied across the territory, especially in low-performing offices.
- Develop relationships with physician and non-physician KOLs. Invite reps into those relationships to help them grow and learn.
- Conduct quality training on sales skills and evaluate to ensure successful learning and adoption of new practices.
- Boost engagement scores and decrease turnover. Rep turnover is currently 27% in the northwest compared to the company average of 15%.

Do not reuse similar Efforts across multiple Deliverables. That will exaggerate the impact of that one Effort across the whole Cipher. This will be discussed more in the Rigor Testing chapter.

Creating the Efforts for the Team and Culture Deliverables

As discussed in the Deliverables chapter, the nuance and specificity of the Team and Culture Deliverables come to life in the Efforts. Furthermore, this is where people make some of the biggest mistakes. Both areas require a level of *radical truth and transparency* that many find uncomfortable.

Let's say on the team side, out of the eight direct reports this person will inherit, two are good, four are just barely average, and two will need to be exited.

That might be hard to admit, but honesty is essential, as the team manager must be able to rebuild this team. Therefore, you must assess candidates' ability to "Upgrade two employees in rapid succession and then quickly evaluate other employees for development and/or upgrading."

The nature of the management approach required is also important to clarify here. The type of management varies greatly depending on the nature of the team, as well as the industry, level, etc. Compare and contrast the variations from in-office vs. trades-based roles, local vs. global responsibilities, or customer-facing vs. operational teams, and you'll quickly realize that a method that works for one group may fall flat if tried with a very different group.

The same can be valid on the culture side. Perhaps you've been trying to implement a flatter culture that espouses empowerment, collaboration, and an ability to question regardless of title, but you've historically been hierarchical and silo-driven. Don't evaluate the candidate solely against the aspirational culture if they must thrive in your current culture first. Instead, assess their ability to tolerate your old culture while helping champion the change to the culture you want for the future.

In that spirit, the following questions will help you think more critically about what will be required for success in this role as you build the Team and Culture Efforts.

Team Management Effort questions to consider:

- How strong and stable is the team right now? Will the new person need to lead an existing high-performing team, develop a junior high-potential team, or upgrade a considerable portion of the group?
- What is the overall managerial complexity and experience/skillset required here? What is the size of the team? How dispersed is it, and what is the mix of geography? Are there a wide range of nationalities and "traditional cultural" differences that have to be managed together? Are there "legacy company" cultural differences? Is this a role for a general manager with a wide array of diverse functions reporting into them?

- Is this a team that requires a hands-on, top-down "command and control" leadership style, or a "team of equals" that operate flatly according to the manner that works best for each individual? For example, think Army vs. two-person consulting partnership.

- What's the emotional state of the team? How is the morale and esprit de corps? And how must that change?

Culture Effort questions to consider:

- How much autonomy is truly provided and embraced in the culture instead of requiring close coordination and connection with others?

- What is the intensity of the workweek like? How much value is placed on work/life/family balance vs. face time in the office requirements?

- Is the whole company geographically contained, or is everyone remote and dispersed?

- Would you consider the culture to be customer-oriented or product-oriented?

- What are the specific values or other behaviors that describe how work actually gets done here?

The Culture Fit Deliverable will typically need at least five, if not more, Efforts to truly capture what is unique and specific about the culture of your company and department.

Craig's real-world story

Due to the nature of the roles we personally assess, we often build our Ciphers with people more removed from the trenches, like a board member or a CEO who has elevated up out of the day-to-day. They give us critical strategic direction but, due to the nature of their role, they may be less connected to the operational details.

Not surprisingly, at times this has created a gap when the Cipher isn't specific enough. Conversely, if we start with those closest to the job, sometimes the Cipher is too operational in nature and may miss the bigger picture.

We have found that when we combine the strategic direction the board offers with the insights provided by peers or the team of the role we're assessing for, we achieve the greatest success. Once the strategic challenge has been set, the secondary conversations give us a view into the Efforts, and sometimes the Deliverables, required for success.

This is where asking for help can be quite valuable. As you develop a Cipher, consider engaging your manager for assistance with articulating a high-level Charge and/or Outcome beyond your immediate needs. Ask your peers or direct reports to comment on the specific Deliverables and Efforts required for someone to succeed in this role.

Aesop's modern fable

Robert Townsend is recognized as the driving force behind the success of Avis Car Rental. Townsend became the CEO in 1962, taking on the challenge of leading a company that had yet to make a profit in thirteen years. By 1965, Avis had increased its sales by 150% and had annual profits of $1 million.[18]

It was well known that the CEO required every leader to know the car rental business inside and out—and that every Avis executive was required to wear the iconic Avis red jacket and work at a rental desk regularly.

Townsend believed in the value of teams, speaking in a manner that got to the heart of an issue and rolling up his sleeves to work alongside his business partners. His focus on understanding how the core business actually operated, and insisting that his team knew as well, helped fuel their success.

Key chapter takeaways

- The Efforts are the prioritized elements that define how each Deliverable will be achieved.
- Working in the trenches often provides the insight to identify the Efforts needed to succeed in a role accurately. (And if you haven't been in the trenches recently, make sure to ask someone who has!)
- There are specific questions you can ask to define the Team and Culture Deliverables in your Cipher creation.

Read it, think it, do it

Continue building out your Cipher.

Identify your top Deliverable from the list in the previous section, and for that top Deliverable, write down the four Efforts most necessary to achieving success.

Repeat this process for your other Deliverables.

Double-check your work:

- Within the Efforts listed, have you clearly defined how success in this Deliverable will be *measured*?
- Have you specified all the critical details of how success will be *achieved*?
- Did you identify what is unique (in this role and company) for each Deliverable?

Cipher Efforts Worksheet	hirebest
The top Deliverable	
Effort #1	
Effort #2	
Effort #3	
Effort #4	
Effort #5	

« PART III: Cipher Refinement »

It's the little details that are vital. Little things make big things happen.

John Wooden, basketball coaching icon

Chapter Eight

Cipher Strengthening

Congratulations! If you've been following along with the "Read it, think it, do it" exercises, you now have the makings of your Cipher, with a Charge, Outcome, and set of Deliverables, and have built out the Efforts for at least one of those Deliverables.

Cipher Strengthening

Choosing your Hiring Board of Advisors

+

Brainstorming with the team

If you want to fully build out your Cipher while reading this book, now would be a perfect time to create the Efforts for the rest of your Deliverables. This will bring you to a complete draft version of your Cipher.

Completing Cipher Strengthening (this chapter) and Rigor Testing (next chapter) can then help you take this initial draft from "good start" to "excellent output"!

Cipher Strengthening is asking for help, in a structured manner, to make sure your Cipher is focused on the correct Outcome with the appropriate Deliverables required. You will engage your manager (and other stakeholders) to ensure alignment on this critical hire. We've seen too many hiring processes resulting in mis-hires because the individual leading the process thought they knew (or had to know) all the answers themselves.

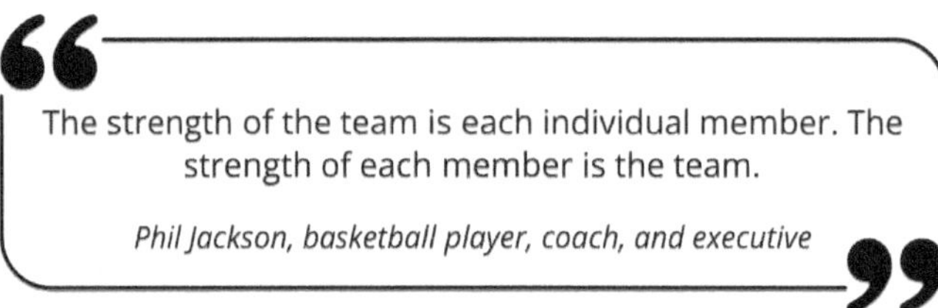

The strength of the team is each individual member. The strength of each member is the team.

Phil Jackson, basketball player, coach, and executive

In the next chapter on Rigor Testing, you will pressure test the final document. Rigor Testing ensures that the final product "makes sense" and avoids many of the pitfalls I have seen in my work. But more on that later.

For Type-A readers, I can feel your energy through the paper, and I know you want to skip these steps...please don't!

The extra hour or two you invest in Strengthening and Rigor Testing your Cipher has a massive ROI. You will be better equipped to hire the right person and thus avoid performance management issues six months later. When you balance those two hours against the time required to manage and eventually fire the person you mis-hire, launch a new search, and hire the right person next time, these steps are truly a no-brainer.

As *another* benefit, involving stakeholders tees up the new hire for success with these individuals. If your colleagues have been involved in designing the role, they have implicitly bought into the expectations for the position. Often, they will be more predisposed to supporting the new employee structurally as they come up to speed–they will feel a sense of ownership, and maybe obligation, to help make that person more successful.

If the role will provide service to internal customers, consider engaging these individuals/teams as stakeholders in both Cipher building and interviewing.

Choosing your Hiring Board of Advisors

In Chapter One, the three reasons the current hiring process fails was discussed. The second reason was that hiring managers usually execute the process in a silo, taking too much upon themselves to get it right. Part of that happens during the interview process, and another occurs during the Cipher development process.

You want to get the right feedback from the people who know the job requirements best. Sometimes, that is you. Often, it's not entirely you. Don't let your ego get in the way—it is okay to ask for help.

For mid- and senior-level positions, multiple people often interact with them, all with their own opinions of what the role should deliver. For example, consider the role of a lawyer in an organization. Some view them as the chief protector from all outward ills, others see their job as completing contracts, while others look to them for internal compliance and risk mitigation strategies. There is no right answer; but be sure that the Cipher requirements and the key stakeholder expectations are aligned.

We call these stakeholders your Hiring Board of Advisors. Let's determine who you should include in that. The first three individuals/archetypes listed below are mission critical, with the rest of the groups to be considered thoughtfully:

1. The hiring manager

Presumably, as you are the one reading this book and drafting a Cipher as you go along, this is you. As an aside, the hiring manager *should* be the one who creates the Cipher. The Cipher is not a document that can be provided to the hiring manager; this individual must be driving the process. If you are a high-performing Talent Acquisition professional building a Cipher based on a rigorous interview of the hiring manager and key stakeholders, that is the one exception. However, if you create a Cipher for someone else, with minimal engagement other than the last job description and an email saying, "C'mon, you know me better than anyone else..." you (and they) should have far less confidence in the result.

2. The hiring manager's manager

This is another critical must-have member, as ultimately this person will evaluate the hiring manager and their team on their ability to accomplish their results. They need to be bought into the type of talent being added to accomplish that. Additionally, senior leaders often have more hands-on experience developing teams and have seen more talent decisions get made (and fail!). We've unfortunately seen too many hiring processes stall when the hiring manager hasn't included their manager in the process, and they "veto" the finalist candidate due to a fundamental disagreement about the role. In many of those situations, a quick roughly 30 minute conversation would have saved countless hours of work chasing after the wrong outcome.

3. Your HR partner(s)

Depending on your company, you may have no help at all, a dedicated recruiting/talent acquisition function, access to one thinly stretched HR person for the entire company, and everything in between. So, I won't tell you to run blindly to HR. But, I will say that you'll benefit greatly from the kind of HR Cipher partner who will push back against potential errors. They should also be able to offer advice on the corporate standard for certain aspects of the role, such as particular expectations for the level you are hiring for, culture/values to be assessed, or other specific criteria that need to be included.

4. Internal customers and/or your peers

In today's more collaborative companies, getting your peers' points of view can create a better end product while building stronger relationships. For example, if you are the VP of Finance, your peers might be the VP of Sales, the VP of Marketing, and the VP of Operations. Ask them what they think this role could further enhance in the Finance department or what is mission-critical about how this role currently interacts with them. For example, perhaps they want your team to provide greater financial analysis and support, and you need someone to bring those skills.

5. Your direct reports/their future peers

Depending on the position level, including direct reports in the process can make a lot of sense. These individuals may be closer to the day-to-day work needed and can shed light on what they need in a colleague. What is it that you didn't see in the last person that they can help you avoid the next time? Similarly, if you are an investor reading this book and thinking about a CEO role in one of your portfolio companies, consider engaging the leadership team (if it's known that the CEO is transitioning.) The company's CFO, CCO, and COO can be invaluable input providers to ensure your hiring process is spot on.

6. External stakeholders

This group can also be considered in select circumstances. For example, if you are hiring for a sales position with a heavy focus on account management, including your top two or three long-term customers in a discussion of what they think is most needed in the role could be helpful. An added benefit is that it shows an interest in their insight that can further strengthen your partnership.

Brainstorming with the team

Once you have built your dream team, it is time to engage them! However, how you approach each team member matters–if you ask the right way, you will receive invaluable insight. But if you ask it the wrong way, you will waste everyone's time with a check-the-box exercise and receive marginal input at best.

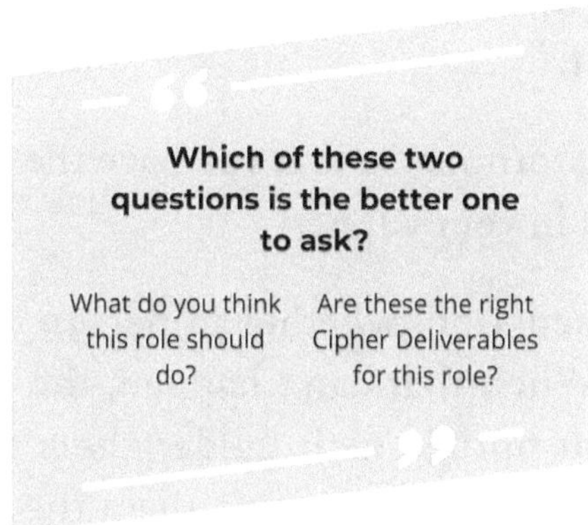

So, what is the right way?

When I run this as a poll question in our training, most people choose the second answer, *"Are these the right Cipher Deliverables for this role?"* After all, you're asking some important people for a favor and want to minimize the burden on them. The problem is...

Most people get it wrong. The correct answer is, "What do you think this role should do?"

Asking, "Are these the right Cipher Deliverables?" is the wrong question because, if you're asking that, it means that you already shared the Deliverables with them. As a result, you've started to limit their thinking to the way *you* see the role. What you really want from them is an answer to how *they* see the role; that's how you'll get independent advice on what matters most.

In our experience, when you present a nearly completed document to a busy person who is juggling reviewing your Cipher with other priorities, they tend to make some light edits but otherwise bless it.

Encourage brainstorming so that you have the best elements of the role included in your Cipher!

This is a live discussion, whether in person or via videoconference/phone. When that can't happen, the HireBest app is another excellent option, as it guides them to provide their unbiased input first before showing them the Cipher for their review. Using email is not recommended; using email dramatically increases the risk that you will get a cursory, "Looks great to me," as they sift through the 99 other emails they need to process that day.

To get the most from them, consider beginning your conversation with the following four elements before you share your Cipher draft:

1. **Explain how come you've asked for their help.** "I asked for your help because I value your input, and specific to this role, because [explain why you chose them]. I'd like to get your quick reactions to a couple of questions before we dive into it, if that's okay?"

2. **Ask for their opinion on the biggest value this person will add?** "When you think about what we need in a [the role you are hiring for], what is the most critical change to the business you hope this person will drive? How does [the business] need to be different as a result of hiring them?"

3. **Ask for more specificity—how will we know when this person has succeeded?** "If we had to use one specific measure to decide whether we hired the right person, thinking a couple of years from today, what would that metric be? What does success look like in your eyes?"

4. **Ask for their advice on the three biggest steps needed to achieve that value and success.** "Given what you've said thus far, what are the two or three most essential Deliverables or things they will need to do to achieve that change?"

Superb! You now have an unbiased view of what they believe matters to the role. Now share your Cipher with them for direct feedback.

Discuss whether and how to resolve differences between their unguided input and what you have created. Openly debate where there are opposing views and reach aligned resolution.

Finally, in the last minutes of the meeting, challenge your advisor to ensure you have everything included. Consider some of the questions below to help spark some new ideas.

- What else would you hope this person would do?
- In a perfect world, what responsibilities would you want this person to take on if you knew you'd find someone who could do it?
- What are you most unhappy about regarding the current incumbent's performance, and what do you hope the new employee will do differently?

Note: in roughly a quarter of the brainstorming sessions we facilitate, we find the last question will uncover a new Deliverable that is more important than anything we have already.

After the meeting: re-prioritize and winnow down

Perhaps you created a solid list of five or six Deliverables. Then, you engaged critical team members and collectively added another few — getting your total up to eight or nine. Now, you must get this number down to a manageable six or seven, the sweet spot for a Cipher. This is to keep the practical limit of how many Deliverables an interviewer can evaluate. It also creates a set of responsibilities that a new employee can realistically focus on and achieve.

Refining and prioritizing your Cipher is a critical step in the process. Put the document away for a bit and come back to it, engaging in a bit of reflection. Ask yourself, where are you saying the same thing in different ways? Where are the underlying traits and characteristics the same? Finally, what is absolutely critical vs. what is really a "nice to have" item.

Craig's real-world story

We had a client looking for a new CEO, and they called us in towards the end of their search when they were down to their final two candidates. Unfortunately, only two of the four board members could make the Cipher creation meeting. Regardless, we met with the two members, and they emphasized operational execution, recent customer acquisition, and M&A growth.

As we refined the Cipher around their perspective, we connected back with the other two members of the board, who said the most important need was to review the strategy deeply because they believed the strategy was very much in flux. In contrast, the first two members of the team thought the strategy was nailed down. This led to an added board meeting to discuss the new CEO's mandate so that the board was more aligned with the organization's future strategy.

Ultimately, this conversation drove a completely different focus in who they needed to hire. Our assessment showed that one candidate was far better strategically than the other. The team chose the more strategic CEO; that person helped the company recognize and react to a challenging strategic development in the market. If we didn't ensure that all key stakeholders were aligned on the Cipher, the second candidate would have come out ahead but would have been the wrong hire for them because that person did not have the ability to execute on a critical Deliverable (strategy development).

Aesop's modern fable

When Mary Barra took over as General Motors chairperson and CEO in 2014, she was called a "lightweight" by a Wall Street investment banker. Since her appointment, Barra has been anything but, guiding GM through its post-bankruptcy recovery, leading through widespread vehicle recalls and public relations crises, and helping the company make a consistent profit.

Barra is known for using inclusive leadership to garner employee advocates and improve business operations. She sprinted to revamp the 2012 Chevrolet Malibu, quickly making changes that improved sales.

During the auto crisis, she increased efficiency through product innovation and created more vehicles with the same parts. She also helped align GM's purchasing and product development departments, which had previously never been done.[19]

Her predecessor, Dan Akerson, said she brought order to the chaos of GM's expansive product development function through her natural ability to engage others. She earned credibility through her track record of bringing new models to market faster and at a lower cost.

She took her vision to the top spot at GM and found success as a consensus builder who brought teams together to solve the organization's most critical challenges.[20]

Key chapter takeaways

- No one can do it all on their own! Your Cipher will be far better if you take a collaborative approach and involve key stakeholders.
- Your Hiring Board of Advisors needs to include, at a minimum, the hiring manager, the hiring manager's manager, and your HR partners.
- Use open-ended questions at take a brainstorming approach as you capture stakeholder perspectives.
- Take the time to reflect on the feedback and to refine and re-prioritize your Cipher.

Read it, think it, do it

Meet with at least one of your advisors and gain their input into your Cipher.

How did their framing of what is needed in the role match your Charge and Outcome? How was it different?

How did the conversation strengthen your Deliverables? Which ones, if any, were eliminated in favor of some of theirs?

What was the most significant value you received from the conversation?

How could their input and the conversation be even better next time? How would you change this process?

Chapter Nine

Rigor Testing

Have you ever spent a lot of time creating something you took great pride in, or that you believed looked genuinely magnificent? Most of us have.

Many of us have also returned to it later and experienced something between complete unfamiliarity and absolute horror: how did the masterpiece we remember turn into the mess now before us?

Rigor Testing

Exclusivity

Decision Rights

A/B Testing

Deal Breakers

The Good Lens

Rigor Testing essentially formalizes that "fresh mind" review to ensure that the finished document is one you are truly proud of and accurately reflects what you need in the role.

For pragmatic readers who are worried that these are simply the extra suspenders to the prior belt of Cipher Strengthening and, therefore, believe they can skip this step, let me explain how these two topics are quite different.

In Cipher Strengthening, you learned the value of engaging our Hiring Board of Advisors to go beyond our thoughts to strengthen our Cipher. This was the implementation of 1 + 1 = 3, or two heads are better than one, but it is still subject to the risk of confirmation bias.

For example, as you actively create the Cipher and remain engaged, your brain might stay stuck in the overall framework of how you are thinking about the role. Therefore, additions and subtractions are weighed against your original perspective. You may evolve the document from current thinking, but fundamentally, you are still viewing it through the same lens you used when creating it.

Rigor Testing provides a fresh lens to evaluate your Cipher so you can see it as others will.

The five components of Rigor Testing

We offer five quick Rigor Tests to confirm (or revise) the critical assumptions about the role you are hiring for. In total, this should be a 30-to-45-minute exercise that will save you multiples of that time by avoiding a mistake in hiring.

When building Ciphers for clients, I instinctively check for these things as part of our process. Once you have created several Ciphers (and started to become a Cipher master), you will find you can do this too. But as you start using the tool, you need to build your mastery toolkit by explicitly following these five Rigor Tests every time until you have achieved muscle memory.

I will discuss how to conduct each Rigor Test in each section below. But first, the question is *when you should do the Rigor Test.* The answer is *not right away.*

We strongly suggest that you conduct Rigor Testing no earlier than the day following the creation of your Cipher. Let it sit overnight and look at it with fresh eyes the following day to get the most value out of the exercise. The mental break between creation and Rigor Testing enables you to uncover effectively where your thesis has missing parts or where you glossed over critical components.

Enough about the set-up. Let's learn how this is done!

1. Exclusivity

The first Rigor Test is the most important. The Exclusivity Rigor Test helps you avoid one of the primary decision mistakes people make. If you recall from our three Deliverable rules, Exclusivity means that every Deliverable can be assessed independently of the other Deliverables. By following this rule, you avoid the situation where one element of a candidate's experience or a single character trait influences multiple sections of your Cipher rating.

Consider the following scenario: many people today work in some form of a matrixed organization where collaboration and relationship building are essential. Therefore, in a Cipher for a new Director of Customer Success, the hiring manager may want to emphasize the need to build the strategy collaboratively, to partner with Sales to analyze performance and metrics, to build and develop internal relationships to resolve customer issues, and to manage shared resources in conjunction with peers.

While there is an element of truth to all four of those requests, once you begin assessing a candidate, that individual starts to shine or tarnish across all four parts based largely on their ability to collaborate. You may find yourself hiring someone who is an excellent collaborator but average on all the other aspects of the role.

To avoid the scenario described above, you would want to make sure that each Deliverable is focused on the actual underlying skill or accountability. An example would be to have "Analyze performance and metrics" as its own Deliverable, separate from a new Deliverable of "Work collaboratively with Sales, Operations, and other functional peers." This allows you to make clear trade-offs regarding a candidate's actual abilities on "analysis" vs. "collaboration." For instance, I have met candidates who are collegial and friendly but otherwise ineffectual, and the inverse, cold and abrasive but wildly effective and efficient in driving bottom-line results. Separating the skills from the behavioral style allows you to make a better decision.

How to test

First, review each Deliverable and its corresponding Efforts and look for any obvious overlap from one Deliverable to another. If simple, unintentional, overlapping areas can be quickly addressed, then do so. Otherwise, highlight it and return to it after the second part of the test.

The second part of the test is to go through the mental exercise of grading the Cipher for a hypothetical candidate. Consider what interview responses and data you will need to gain conviction in their ability to succeed on the Efforts and compare that across each of the Deliverables. Hopefully, you will see minimal overlap in the type of data you want for the first Deliverable vs. the second, and so on. If you find yourself envisioning the same sort of data across multiple Deliverables, then you are at a major risk of violating the Exclusivity principle. Consider this checklist as a starting point for your process (and the goal is to be able to answer "No" to each of the questions):

- Are there particular buzzwords or stylistic approaches replicated across multiple Deliverables?
- Are any of your Efforts the same across multiple Deliverables? Often the same Effort is included in a couple of Deliverables in the first draft.
- Would this Effort fit into multiple Deliverables as easily as it does in the one you initially assigned it to? (If so, it may belong in a universal Deliverable of Team Management or Culture or even somewhere else entirely.)
- Will the ratings on multiple Deliverables be affected by their performance on just one of them?
- Based on your prediction of the data an ideal candidate would have for one Deliverable, are the skills and attributes you hope to see identical to a different Deliverable?

Tweak to resolve

Resolving exclusivity issues requires careful consideration so you don't break one Deliverable by fixing another. Challenge yourself to be as specific as possible within the Deliverable to get to the heart of how to accomplish your Outcome.

As you tighten the language and move Efforts around, consider whether you should be adding Efforts to other Deliverables or re-prioritizing and cutting Efforts as part of the cleanup. Do you really need that duplication of Efforts, or can you simply eliminate the overlap? Or can you combine two Deliverables into one, because upon reflection, you were simply looking at the same need, just from two different angles?

2. Decision Rights

Decision Rights are where the rubber meets the road in determining whether you want a *doer* to help execute your directives or a *leader* to create the plan and achieve the results.

For many overworked leaders, the latter sounds quite appealing, "I just want someone to get this done and make my life manageable." Yet hiring someone at too high or too low a level compared to your real needs can be disastrous.

It is critical to ensure that you have the right match between the autonomy you expect to provide and the autonomy they will demand. Especially with front-line managers and mid-level hires up to the executive level, I often see expectations around decision-making as the crux of friction. Getting this wrong results in either a too-senior hire who becomes discouraged and ends up quitting or, conversely, a too-junior resource constantly checking in for permission before making any move.

Similar to the guidance provided in earlier chapters about ensuring that your Culture Deliverable reflects *the way things are today* vs. *how you aspire them to be*, the same is true regarding Decision Rights. Do you want someone who can fully own a problem, identify potential solutions, and drive one of them to resolution in a self-directed manner? Or do you really want someone who will support you with close involvement and interaction from yourself?

How to test

Simply look at each Deliverable and consider what decisions will be needed to achieve it. Then, question yourself; are you ready to truly empower the person to make that call? The following question really helps clarify the level of decision authority you are willing to provide:

(After they have been in the role for six months and come up to speed): When would I want to know about a decision this individual will need to make to achieve the Deliverable?

Ideally, your answer aligns with the Efforts that support the Deliverable.

As an illustration, if your Efforts and Deliverables read as though you are looking for a highly autonomous leader who will decide on the correct approach and implement it, then you should be comfortable having some awareness that a decision is in process but not be overly involved.

Conversely, suppose you answer that you want to know as they launch the project, to be involved as they consider potential options, and to be updated along the way generally. In that case, your Deliverables and Efforts should reflect someone who assembles data and synthesizes options for your consideration and decision.

Tweak to resolve

This one is straightforward: adjust the Efforts and Deliverables to reflect whether you are empowering them with decision rights or asking them to inform your decision. At the same time, ensure you are thinking across the entire timeline of the Cipher and Outcome.

A common mistake is to build the Cipher based on the level of decision involvement you want in the early days (when they are learning the role) vs. two to six months later when they have established themselves. If you want someone who will own the decision and accept your input as they get up to speed, note that within the Efforts.

As an aside, based on examining thousands of leaders, I strongly encourage you to resist the urge to deepen your involvement in the day-to-day by getting someone too junior. Instead, challenge yourself to accept the need for greater autonomy, supply more decision authority, and as a result, accelerate business performance.

3. A/B Testing

A/B Testing verifies that your Deliverables are appropriately prioritized amongst each other. While specific weights to Deliverables are not applied (to avoid creating a sense of false precision), you are strongly encouraged to order them from most to least important. The one exception to this is the Culture Deliverable; in most cases, you should put Culture at the end of the list. Not because it is not important; rather, it is so important that it should be at the end so it does not get lost in the middle.

How to test

Looking only at the top two Deliverables, imagine a choice of Candidate A, who did exceptionally well on the first but not the second, and Candidate B, who did exceptionally well on the second but not the first. With no further information to go on, who do you hire?

If you choose Candidate A, then you have prioritized correctly. If you think you would prioritize Candidate B, you need to flip the order and bump your first Deliverable down into the second position. Now continue down your list of Deliverables, making sure that two would be preferred to three, three preferred over four, and so forth.

Tweak to resolve

The simple beauty of this test is that you have already fixed it once you have tested! As you went through, you should have adjusted them into the right order already as you moved Deliverables down and up based on which one was more important.

4. Deal Breakers

The Deal Breakers rigor test is deeply related to A/B Testing, and for the most part, the testing you did before likely identified any of these already. As you work through the A/B Testing process, you may realize that an ability, skill, or character trait is a critical must-have in your next candidate, typically because there is almost no way a person could be successful in the role without it. This is something that, regardless of their other strengths, will stop you from hiring them if they don't have this ability. This item may not be in Deliverable #1, but is so foundational that it needs to be called out.

For example, a Software Engineer's knowledge of a particular programming language may be a Deal Breaker. It is entirely acceptable to demand expertise in Perl or Java if you cannot take the time to train someone in the language. Yet the number one Deliverable may be architecting the software strategy for a particular product.

On the sales side, maybe the Deal Breaker is a substantive network of contacts in a particular geography or industry.

In both examples, the Deal Breaker is a seemingly minor item compared to the strategic needs of the role. This is why you should not re-order your Deliverables, but rather to call it out as an absolute necessity in the Cipher.

Fundamentally, the Deal Breaker test is thinking through critical driving directions and prioritization decisions that you must catalog today to shorten the search cycle and avoid compromising on something essential in the role.

How to test

There is minimal extra work to be done for this Rigor Test other than to reflect on what you've just done with the A/B Testing and ensure that you have fully captured any strong reactions you had about prioritization.

Deal Breakers tend to fall out naturally. Somewhere around your third or fourth Deliverable, you find that the overall Deliverable is in the middle in terms of prioritization but that a specific need must be filled. It doesn't require changing the prioritization, yet it becomes clear that a candidate without this ability or trait will not work.

Tweak to resolve

For most Deal Breakers, consider adding a note to tell the recruiters which Effort is a "must have" item to screen for. At the same time, consider bouncing your list of Deal Breakers off of a key stakeholder or HR professional to ensure you have not inserted bias as well as impossible requirements into your search.

Avoid creating too many deal breakers, especially around a specific experience level. Some of the best-performing candidates we've seen lacked explicit, proven ability on an Effort but had a proven track record of success on underlying elements that would predict future success.

It is worth repeating how important it is for you to communicate these Deal Breakers to whomever is helping you source and screen candidates. Identifying these attributes can dramatically cut down on the amount of time wasted with candidates who will never be able to succeed in the role.

5. The Good Lens

The Good Lens recalls the lesson from Aesop (not us, the original guy from Greece): "Be careful what you wish for; you might just get it." Ask yourself:

- If you could find someone who excelled at each of your Deliverables and your Outcome, is that someone you would want to hire and work with?
- How likely is it that you can find and/or afford that person?
- When clients are asked this question, their face says it all: "Of course, I want to hire them. They do all the things I said I wanted!"

The issue is that you have defined the forest by describing the five to seven Deliverable trees. The combination of those character traits and/or strengths may not be the right individual you want to actually work with. Even within a specific Deliverable, the underlying requirements to be successful might be someone who doesn't fit within the culture or otherwise would not make for a good team member.

The Good Lens allows you to consider who you have defined as the ideal person in the context of the overall role and the organization.

How to test

Once more, return to an examination of your Cipher.

Walk through each Deliverable, noting the type of experience a person would need to show to earn a top rating. You are defining "good," which will also be helpful when you begin interviewing (more on this later).

Picture that person in your mind: given your specific role/industry, what is reasonable to expect someone to show against that Deliverable? Suppose you are hiring a customer service manager in an organization with well-developed policies. In that case, a Deliverable of "Ensure consistent and top-quality service delivery" will require someone to come up to speed quickly on what policies matter for your company and to maintain them. Therefore, stories of entering new organizations and understanding what mattered for success, teaching that to their teams, and enforcing it when people deviated are all things you hope to hear in the interview.

With "good" defined, then ask:

- Does that accurately describe the type of person I believe works well here? Does the "how" and "what" of the Deliverables and Efforts align with the company's culture?
- Are these Deliverables, both individually and in aggregate, reasonable to expect one person to achieve? (One test: could you have done all of these a few years back? Would you have made the cut?)
- What is the market compensation for someone with that experience, and how does it compare to my budget?

Tweak to resolve

Like Decision Rights, the resolution is to adjust the Deliverables and/or Efforts in those places where you now realize the Cipher does not reflect what you want. Your intuition will get you most of the way.

If you are stuck, return to your Hiring Board of Advisors and ask their opinion. Bosses and HR are especially valuable, as both groups often have a more comprehensive understanding of what might be reasonable to expect for a given role. Additionally, an HR or a search partner can often provide a rough sense of what talent might be available to you (either internally or in the current market).

Defining the Good Lens is exceptionally helpful for your interview process.

By stepping back and considering the experience, details, and qualifications a person needs to earn a top rating, you internalize precisely what you are looking for. You will be able to move much quicker to sort out those who don't "have it" and run fast to hire the person who does.

When you align with your hiring team while preparing for interviews, you can describe exactly what constitutes a top rating so they can accurately and independently rate the candidate.

Craig's real-world story

Earlier, I discussed the value of waiting to Rigor Test until a day or two after you have created the Cipher. The following is an example of the benefit of Rigor Testing the Cipher even several months into a search.

A client searching for a new CEO believed commercial orientation was the most crucial characteristic to predict success. Their Cipher focused on that as not only a key Deliverable but also as a crucial part of the Charge.

Based on this assumption, none of the candidates met expectations. While they found strong commercial candidates, none fared well on the operational aspects of the role, which was lower in priority.

Something stopped our client from moving forward, as they believed that the customers of this company would demand far more operational expertise from a CEO than what their candidates presented with.

After reviewing another batch of seemingly impressive resumes from one of the top search firms, and ruling most of them out, I took a step back and questioned what they were really looking for in the role.

After some consideration, it was clear that operational leadership needed to be prioritized as one of the top Deliverables, which triggered a reconsideration of the Charge itself.

With a refined Cipher, the company hired an incredibly successful CEO. This CEO oversaw operational improvements, which led to better sales performance (as customers were happier with the product), leading to substantial growth for the company.

Aesop's modern fable

It's a story that's been told repeatedly: Steve Jobs completely turned Apple on its head upon his return to the company in 1997. He slashed the company's bloated product line and provided everyone from the top down with a unified vision. With Jobs at the helm, innovation and design excellence became the company-wide priorities. In short order, Jobs' (admittedly obsessive) attention to detail began permeating all aspects of Apple's operations.

This visionary viewed every detail, from the shape of the icons on the iPhone to the type of materials used in Apple retail stores, as a critical driver of commercial success that called for deep thought and consideration.

While I have never had the opportunity to work with Mr. Jobs, I am fairly confident he would be a fan of the Rigor Testing approach. The rigor he brought to his design approach pushed Apple into its position as a global force.

Key chapter takeaways

- When making critical decisions, "good enough" rarely is. Running 25 miles of the marathon doesn't count, so finish the last mile strong with your Cipher Rigor Testing!
- Rigor Testing is different from Cipher Strengthening. Rigor Testing provides a new set of lenses to pressure test your Cipher.
- There are five Rigor Tests, each with a prescribed process for testing and tweaking. These include:
    - Exclusivity
    - Decision Rights
    - A/B Testing
    - Deal Breakers
    - The Good Lens

Read it, think it, do it

As encouraged, cajoled, and implored above, take the time to run through these five Rigor Tests for your Cipher.

Make a note of which ones were beneficial and changed your perspective versus those you could easily breeze through.

For your next few Ciphers, make notes each time. Do you see a pattern emerging? If so, consider how to evolve your process to avoid getting caught by those Rigor Tests.

« PART IV: Using the Cipher to Improve Talent »

Action is the foundational key to all success.

Pablo Picasso, painter, sculptor, and printmaker

Chapter Ten

Grading your Cipher

Welcome to Part IV—using the Cipher. Your investment in defining the role in the prior chapters is about to pay off. If you just stopped here, you would get tremendous value from using this framework. You could identify candidates who genuinely fit what you need, waste less time with candidates who are mismatched for the company, and be far more aligned with your manager and internal clients on what success looks like in this role.

To truly HireBest, you will grade the candidate objectively against the Cipher requirements using the data you collect in interviews.

The Cipher keeps your interview team aligned and focused on the prioritized Deliverables during their interviews. They can now look for data that fits what you're looking for in the role rather than simply getting to know a nice person who might not have the right experience.

While I won't go into great depth on conducting an interview here, I want to leave you with a solid understanding of using your Cipher to grade candidates effectively.

As an aside, if you are not already using a structured interview, you should be. Hundreds of research studies have consistently proven that a structured approach, with a consistent set of questions and approach to asking the questions, results in significantly stronger hiring results and greater legal defensibility of your hiring process!

If you want to learn how to conduct structured interviews, check out our online resources.You can take a demo course, try out an on-demand offering, or even inquire about a live course.

It's all about data

Whether you explicitly ask questions aligned against the Cipher you've created, or have learned to listen for the right answers from open-ended and unaided questions, the key is getting the right data. This allows you to predict accurately whether this individual can create the type of impact you are looking for. You should make sure your interview process is designed to get the candidate to fully present their abilities against the Cipher, but *without ever showing them or telling them the Cipher.*

This is not the time for gut-level reactions like "I feel" and "I believe" statements but rather a careful weighing of whether there is enough data to predict future success.

If done correctly, your interview process results in both positive and neutral-to-negative data about the candidate's ability to achieve these Deliverables.

What data should you weigh the heaviest? The one data point about when they messed up so royally that you would never want to see that sort of failure associated with you or your team? The one data point where they knocked it out of the park and blew away expectations?

The answer is no to both.

We would caution you against making any decision based on one data point. You are looking for a pattern throughout the candidate's career. Examine the facts unemotionally and in reference to your Cipher to make the best-informed decision about the candidate's ability to perform in the future.

Create and align the interview team on a grading scale in advance

At Aesop Partners and HireBest, we understand that the truth of life is found somewhere in the gray space. We can almost guarantee you will never find a perfect fit for your Cipher. If you do, we might wonder if your Cipher is truly rigorous enough!

At the same time, at least after passing a first screening, it is rare to find someone who has zero fit against the Cipher. But the key is to match the grays between what you need and what the candidate offers, and that's precisely where grading comes in.

Using a specific grading scale challenges interviewers to make defined choices to measure a particular candidate's strengths and weaknesses accurately.

It is also why I advocate for a four-point scale when grading Ciphers: there is nowhere to hide between a thumbs up or thumbs down. Rather, a decision must be reached on whether the data collected suggests strengths or weaknesses for every Deliverable and Outcome. Our favorite scale is provided below. If you don't have one or don't love the one you have, try it out!

	Sample scale hirebest
4	Prior track record firmly supports strength on this deliverable.
3	The candidate will be able to accomplish most of the efforts within a reasonable range of timeliness.
2	Candidate lacks demonstrated strength against efforts and/or has a mixed record with as much risk as strength.
1	Candidate presented substantial evidence that this will be a critical weakness for them.

Regardless of which scale you use, all interview team members must understand how to use the scale to achieve the best results from your hiring process.

As the hiring manager, you are the person with the greatest stake in this decision; take responsibility for educating the team. Make sure that they understand the Cipher itself. Then, help them know what good looks like *(I told you that the Good Lens would come in handy!)* Consider the following questions as you help prepare them:

- What is the realistic set of data that would merit a top rating?
- What experience would rate someone in the second category vs. the third?
- How much tolerance is there for a few stumbles before someone must get rated down to the third or even fourth category?

As the hiring manager, use your experience and intuition to predict the type of data you would expect from someone who is a high vs. low performer. After all, you have likely worked in your function for several years, so think about the top performers you have known vs. the average vs. the lower and so on. The more you can communicate this to the other interviewers who aren't as skilled as you, the better they can advise your decision.

Evaluate each Deliverable independently

First, note that when grading a Cipher, you start with the Deliverables and then get to the Outcome last. Try not to get too caught up in whether you think this person is good for the job overall; instead, keep focused on a Deliverable-by-Deliverable rating and then assess whether they can do the overall job.

The Rigor Test removed any Exclusivity challenges, so hold firm as you grade your Cipher. Looking at your interview notes, evaluate each Deliverable independently:

- What examples did they share of successfully carrying out something highly similar to the Efforts for this Deliverable?

- Alternatively, what failure examples did they offer related to this Deliverable? Are those recent failures (with no sign of improvement), or long-ago failures that they have learned from and corrected since?

- Is there any evidence to believe this prior pattern won't continue?

- From that data alone, how likely are they to be successful against this Deliverable?

Between each Deliverable, pause and ensure you are ready to assess their performance on the next one independently. It is quite easy to start to trend negatively or positively based on one Deliverable, especially as you first use this method. Make sure you're giving the candidate a fair shot and, ultimately, giving yourself the best chance of finding the right employee for the role you so critically need to fill.

It is not unusual to find someone who rightly deserves a very tough rating on one Deliverable but is quite strong on several others. The lesson here is don't get biased toward a pattern of ratings as you move through the evaluation process.

Do not simply average your scale

Sometimes, despite how hard you try, giving a clean grade for the entire Deliverable is exceedingly tricky. Perhaps they are an absolute rock star on two of the four Efforts and an utter failure on the other two.

While mathematically, the average of 10, 10, 0, and 0 is 5, when evaluating an individual's ability to perform, an average rarely reflects how they will perform.

Consider a couple of different solutions:

- Are the low-performing Efforts so critical that they will stop the successful completion of the entire Deliverable? Perhaps the Deliverable as a whole should be rated in the lowest category.

- Could you envision a scenario where you could carve off responsibility for those low-performing Efforts and assign them elsewhere? Consider splitting this Deliverable into two Deliverables: one they are responsible for executing and one for overseeing someone else executing.

- A third way is to keep the Deliverables together as one but give a split rating (e.g., a rating of 3 & 1), noting that overall, they will be strong on half and weak on half, and note what further discussion or mitigation is needed.

The key to doing this well, and not simply tweaking the Cipher to fit the candidate you've fallen in love with, is to complete this process consistently across all candidates.

Double-check your decision to reconsider the Cipher with an objective third party. Go back to one of your most insightful members of the hiring team and ask their opinion on the adjustment of the Deliverable first, separate from the fact that a particular candidate was firm on one part of the Deliverable and weak on another.

Independently grade the Outcome

Once you have graded the Deliverables, it is time to grade the Outcome. However, Ciphers need "new math." Regardless of what your second-grade teacher told you, some fours *are* worth more than others.

The rating of the Outcome is not simply an average of the Deliverable ratings. It is the assessment of whether they can achieve that Outcome: *the positive impact you want this individual to have on the company.*

Outcome scores should roughly correspond to the different Deliverable grades, but this is not a hard and fast average.

First, you prioritized the list, so the first Deliverable should be weighed more heavily than the last.

Second, a major red flag sometimes appears in one of the lower-priority Deliverables that cannot be overlooked. Maybe it is a deal-breaker element that was missed in a prior interview, or possibly just such a significant misstep that it stops you from being able to predict success across the rest of the role. Ethical considerations tend to be the primary factor in this category, followed closely by concerns regarding integration into the existing culture, a sizable lack of self-awareness, or significant gaps in decision-making.

When in doubt, focus on the data. Can you reliably predict candidate success in both the what and how of this role? If not, do you have evidence of apparent gaps that suggest failure or simply insufficient strength to be comfortable? Put a line in the sand and decide what, if any, further steps are needed to finalize your decision.

Craig's real-world story

As simple as it sounds, even instituting a defined grading scale and discussing it with your team can improve the quality and efficiency of your hiring process. As part of our training course, we routinely ask how many people have a scale they are aligned on with their team, and we never get more than a quarter of the people raising their hands.

But the few who raise their hands ultimately describe some sort of scale like the one shared earlier. They'll often note that the definition and alignment described at the beginning of the chapter have dramatically helped them focus on what matters most to the hiring decision. When the team has to rate specific Deliverables, with a clear scale, they dig deeper for the right data.

Once you've done it a few times, the process trains you to think in specific facts rather than generalities and emotionally driven predictions.

Aesop's modern fable

When Brian Cornell took over as CEO of Target in 2014, he inherited a company reeling from the aftermath of a major security breach, struggling to prove its omnichannel experience with consumers, and asking tough questions about the viability of its Canadian division.

Cornell gathered the data and made tough calls to produce the strategy as the company's top leader, pulling out of Canada and instituting layoffs. Many have noted that his ability to make solid decisions in muddy waters is based on information applied to the future, not earlier patterns or expectations.

He is also viewed by many as an effective leader due to his willingness to consider multiple perspectives, encouraging collaboration, input, and new ideas (much like the processes described in this book).

Cornell has found the right balance between physical stores and digital commerce, going head-to-head with behemoth competitors Amazon and Walmart.

Sales and profits have steadily grown in the last few years, topping Wall Street forecasts and earning Cornell the CNN Business CEO of the Year in December 2019.[21]

Key chapter takeaways

- Use your Cipher and conduct a structured interview to gather the data you need to predict candidate success in the role.
- Rate the Cipher using a pre-defined rating scale and align the interview team on what type of data would lead to each rating on the scale.
- Evaluate each Deliverable independently and, weighing the ratings of each Deliverable, grade the Outcome independently.

Read it, think it, do it

Further develop your grading framework.

How would you describe to team members what each level of the scale might look like for each of the Deliverables you have created for your Cipher?

Chapter Eleven

Data & Structure Remove Bias

No one goes in looking to sabotage the hiring process purposefully due to prejudices. But if you believe that you are bias-free, think again.

Bias, prejudice, heuristics, or thin-slicing are all natural cognitive behaviors that have helped us survive and thrive for thousands of years as a species. Every time I touch that red thing, it's hot, and I get burned. That rustle in the leaves has always been a snake that tries to bite me. If five of us chase one lion, we win; if five of them chase me, not so much.

While cartooned, applying shortcuts to decision-making is hardwired into who we are as human beings.

As professional interviewers, the team at Aesop and HireBest have been trained to manage and mitigate our biases. We have learned that by acknowledging and challenging our innate tendencies, everyone can train their brains to collect the right information to help make the right decision.

Eliminating bias matters

When eliminating bias is discussed, I mean anything that causes you to make a decision based on flawed data. This is how you make the best hiring decision. There are dozens of well-documented examples of why you should focus on the practice of removing bias, but here are a few to consider:

- Having men and women in management positions maximizes profitability. A 2018 McKinsey report stated that companies in the top 25th percentile for gender variety on their executive teams were 21% more likely to see above-average profits.[22]

- Subconscious bias, even at the recruitment level, can hamper an organization. A Yale University study found that male and female scientists, both trained to be objective, were more likely to hire men, consider them more competent than women, and pay them $4,000 more per year than women.[23]

- Another survey found that for every 1% rise in a workforce's gender and cultural variety, there were corresponding increases of 3% and 9% in sales revenue, resp ectively.[24]

- Meanwhile, *Great Place to Work* reports that when employees feel as if they are treated fairly and without bias, they are 9.8x more likely to look forward to going to work, 6.3x more likely to have pride in their work, and 5.4x more likely to want to stay a long time at their company.[25]

How a Cipher inherently eliminates bias

There are three critical components to eliminating bias from your hiring process:

1. Know precisely what you are looking for so you can unemotionally gauge whether the candidate has that experience or skill set

The best way to reduce bias is to remain fastidiously focused on the candidate's specific qualifications against what you need. Resist the urge to get distracted by intriguing but unnecessary skills or other non-job relevant factors. The process of building a Cipher based on what is needed to succeed in this role is the foundational step to removing bias. Using it consistently for all candidates is a natural (and critical) next step.

2. Gather experience data in a structured manner that does not vary based on the person

If you interview three people, and ask them all different questions, how do you know which one is best?

The best bias-reducing interviews rely on a structured set of questions that are asked of all candidates. Society for Human Resources Management (SHRM) experts also suggest that a blind, systematic approach to reviewing applications and resumes will significantly improve the chances of including the most relevant candidates in your interview pool and uncovering some hidden gems.[26]

3. Be bias-enlightened, not bias-blind

I would love to live in a world with no biases, but that's virtually impossible (and way out of scope for this book!) Therefore, the best that most of us can do is to understand and acknowledge where bias might creep into our process and correct for it. As the lead on the hiring process, consider the question, "Where could bias show up in our decisions today?" It is critical to acknowledge openly that everyone has biases (both subconscious and conscious). It's equally vital to hold each other accountable for removing them from the hiring process as much as possible.[27]

This is where debriefing on the interviews with the hiring team and discussing differences in your Cipher grading can help! Pay attention to where bias might exist (e.g., the interview of a recent grad from your same college, physical differences or similarities, shared interests). Then, remind yourself to stick to the interview script, or assess the data knowing that the interviewer may be at risk for applying their own lens to the interview data.

The best hiring decisions come from having a Cipher designed in advance, and following a structured interview process focused on data, not feelings.

This book has principally focused on that first element above: knowing what you're looking for and unemotionally grading the candidate's experience against that. The Cipher is the first step because it is the linchpin; once you know your destination (the Cipher), it's far easier to map your route there (the Interview). Be sure to follow your investment in this topic with further education on running a structured interview process. Check out our course resources at HireBest.ai or other high-quality structured interview training systems.

Nine ways subconscious bias sneaks into the hiring process

To mitigate the impact of our natural biases' on decision-making, everyone must acknowledge them and adjust for them. For those of you who meditate, the approach will feel familiar.

When you notice that a bias has crept into your decision-making, acknowledge it. Now that you see it, name it and move past it. It has lost its power and can slip right back out of your mind.

Over 200 cognitive biases[28] have been identified and explained by experts in the field. As a manager, you do not need to know all of them! But you do need to be able to identify the most common biases that can alter your and your team's decision-making. When biases are not well managed, interviewers subconsciously change interview questions or make assumptions about the data the candidate is sharing.

1. First impressions

Have you ever heard the phrase, "You don't get a second chance to make a good first impression"? You will probably make a judgment about the candidate in the first few minutes of an interview. Unless actively managed, that first impression can become the filter by which you view all subsequent information from the candidate. Managing it is consciously stopping yourself from making any immediate conclusions and always asking, "What does this data tell me?"

2. Nonverbal

The person's appearance, manner, or body language can cause the interviewer to draw inferences about them before or during the interview. In today's videoconference world, you also have to be mindful of reading too much into their home environment or background as well.

If you find yourself making assumptions about a candidate based on nonverbal cues, acknowledge it. Then, look for other data points to help triangulate the finding you think you're reaching. For example, if they look uninterested, notice whether their tone and speech pattern also match. Is all the data they're sharing indicative of someone who isn't interested, or they simply have a different approach to eye contact and you're reading too much into it?

3. Similarity attraction

You're interviewing a candidate, and they are telling you a story about balancing work with their kid's baseball practice. Suddenly, you get these warm and fuzzy feelings, realizing you have something in common with the candidate. While building rapport and finding similarities can help, don't let that deter you from digging in to uncover the data you need to make the right decision. Just because you're awesome, and they like to do the things you want to do, doesn't mean they're awesome too when it comes to what is needed to do the job you are looking to hire for! You still need to finish the interview and find the relevant data.

4. Contrast

We call this the "good enough" bias. This often happens when you have to sift through hundreds of resumes or make a choice across several candidates. You'll naturally compare and contrast. That part is fine. The bias risk is that when one candidate seems better than the others, you are more likely to rate them higher than you would if evaluating them singularly. Ask yourself, "Is this person actually good or just better than the others?" Make sure they are strong and not just the least weak!

5. Halo and horns

Do you find that you are anchored to one particular attribute of a candidate? When you notice that one good (halo) or bad (horns) thing about a person clouds everything else, you have fallen into the halo or horns bias. Just because they struggled at one job does not mean they'll struggle forever, or vice versa.[29] (For those of you who have taken or will take our Mastery course, you'll recognize this bias as the "Bright Spot" and "Lights Out" decision-making traps.) Mitigate this bias by setting aside that one attribute and asking yourself if you would still make the same hiring decision. If not, consider whether that data point should be the deciding factor and make a bias-enlightened decision.

6. Confirmation

This is looking for data and evidence that validate your preconceived notions.[30] Let's assume that your boss is about to make a hiring decision. They generally make great decisions (after all, they hired you) but have asked for your opinion before finalizing the offer letter. When interviewing the candidate, you notice some underperformance in their last job and ask about it. They breezily explained how the market had moved against them, or their goals were set too high, etc., or otherwise make somewhat reasonable excuses to cover it.

Watch out because this is where confirmation bias kicks in. An average interviewer accepts this well-reasoned (and well-rehearsed) answer because it lets them agree with their boss and move on. A master interviewer digs in, recognizing that the overall story doesn't hold up, and comes to their own conclusion regardless of what the other interviewers might think.

7. Action

The bane of many fast-moving people is making a decision based on too little data. They might think, "I don't need a full-hour interview; I know in the first five minutes whether to hire or end it early." Or that they don't need to run through their interview notes and rate the Cipher; they can just give an overall grade. Or that they don't even need a Cipher in the first place; they know what they're looking for. To these people, the hour lost "checking this useless box" feels like a significant investment... until you remind yourself of the time it will take to unravel a hiring mistake.[31]

8. Affect heuristic (optimism and pessimism)

This is a decision-making shortcut based on your affective (emotional) state. This becomes a risk when some event or thought outside of the interview has triggered a strong emotion that changes how you interact with or perceive the candidate. Perhaps this interview was jammed into your schedule at the last minute, and you're angry at the loss of planned working time. Or, before walking in, you learned that the client finally signed the deal worth half of your goal for the month, and everything looks rosy to you. Or even in the interview, perhaps the candidate just used a phrase your ex-spouse used to use! Ensure you're reacting to the candidate, not the baggage you brought into the room.

9. Conformity

Most often occurring in a group or panel interview process, interviewers can be subconsciously swayed by group thinking, whether toward the positive or negative. While I fully support collaborative decision processes and the value of talking through a problem, you must avoid group thinking. During the interview, sticking to pre-planned questions will help. After the interview, avoid discussing the candidate until you have independently rated their performance on the Cipher. Putting your own stake in the ground will help anchor you to your perspective rather than becoming swept up by the views of others.

Note these are not the only nine biases you will encounter as an interviewer, and they are not the only ones that a Cipher-driven approach will reduce. But they are the most common areas where our team most often see managers go astray in hiring.

Craig's real-world story

Before becoming a leadership consultant, I worked at one of the premier management consulting firms, Boston Consulting Group (BCG). BCG taught me that a dedicated team of incredibly smart people, combined with access to the right tools and data, can solve the most demanding challenges that have hindered all the industry experts.

It's also an example of one of the biases that I had to overcome. Because of my background, when assessing fellow alums, it would have been easy to give high marks to anyone from BCG (or McKinsey, Bain, or other top firms). But, that would mean making two decision errors. First, just because these firms hired them does NOT mean they were a good fit; for all I know, recruiting messed up when they hired them! But even if they were the best ever, just because a person is smart and dedicated does not mean they can do any job.

Fortunately, I had mentors who stopped me from making poor decisions based on a candidate's background at a specific organization. Instead, they taught me to consider whether the candidate had demonstrated strengths against a specific company need. I have saved numerous companies from making this exact hiring error as a result.

Aesop's modern fable

If you know anything about that funny sport with the odd-shaped ball they play on a 100-yard field, you've probably heard about Tom Brady. You might even know that he was passed over in his draft. 198 times. When he retired in 2023, he was the only active player from his class.[32] So why did it take six rounds before he was finally drafted? Bias.

This skinny kid with unspectacular arms was a virtual unknown outside the University of Michigan fan base.[33]

An entire cacophony of biases can be seen in the decision to pass over Brady:

- Nonverbal bias. He didn't look like what the scouts thought a quarterback should look like.
- Halo and horns. Since he was too skinny and not as fast as some others, scouts didn't need to look at anything else about him.
- Conformity. No one else was talking about him, so why should a team want him?

Do you remember how great the New England Patriots were before Brady? Me neither. There were far too many years of mediocrity before he came on scene. If you're a fan elsewhere, imagine how much better your favorite team would have been had they looked past their biases and scooped up Tom before the Patriots did.

What if one of the other teams used a Cipher like the one below to attempt the type of analytical decision-making Bill Belichick does so well?

At the time of the 2000 draft, Belichick was relatively new on the job and had left the responsibility of quarterback coaching and acquisition to his most recent hire; he had brought on veteran Dick Rehbein as the QB/Assistant Coach only eight weeks earlier. Even with his extensive experience, Rehbein was new to the QB position and brought no biases to the draft.

Other teams were turned off by Brady's lukewarm career at Michigan and lack of athleticism, but Rehbein's fresh eyes allowed him to pick up the game's greatest player of all time.

<table>
<tr><td colspan="2">Patriot's Pre-Brady Quarterback Cipher </td></tr>
<tr><td colspan="2">Charge: An adept and charismatic QB to lead the New England Patriots franchise back from mediocre results to the glory days.</td></tr>
<tr><td colspan="2">Outcome: Perform individually as an athlete while leading the team to deliver AFC (American Football Conference) championships in two out of three years. Deliver at least one Super Bowl championship within the same three-year window.</td></tr>
<tr><td>Deliverable: Leverage superior athletic ability for success on the field.
Efforts:<ul><li>Pass on time and accurately with superior arm strength and pinpoint accuracy.</li><li>Move quickly enough to escape defenders and extend plays.</li><li>Possess the size and physical stature to handle any throwing lane and be ready to take a pounding.</li><li>Be tough enough to be the ball carrier in short-yardage situations.</li></ul></td><td>Grade: Questionable

Brady could not drive the football sixty yards down the field at significant velocity.

His arm talent, speed, and size were lukewarm during his time at the University of Michigan.</td></tr>
<tr><td>Deliverable: Incorporate intelligence and experience into making the right calls during the heat of battle.
Efforts:<ul><li>Learn and drive the offense with audibles as needed; bring a natural understanding of the game and the team's capabilities.</li><li>Intuitively read the opponent's defensive schemes and anticipate their likely moves.</li><li>Possess a sixth sense connection with receivers</li></ul></td><td>Grade: Acceptable +

There were hints of his capabilities in this dimension during his junior and senior years, especially at the Orange Bowl.

His ability to deliver under pressure and find his receivers was still developing.</td></tr>
</table>

Patriot's Pre-Brady Quarterback Cipher continued	
Deliverable: Develop a humble, continuous improvement system, leading peers as a role model. **Efforts:** • Identify areas for improvement regardless of whether the game was won or lost. • Be completely and unequivocally dedicated to making himself and the team better. • Give 100% effort consistently; able to outwork everyone else. • Stays positive in the face of impossible challenges. Bring a natural understanding of the game and his team's capabilities.	**Grade: Clear Strength** Brady played backup his first two seasons, slowly working his way up to starter. His college coach, Urban Meyer, said, "He never loses...and the number one characteristic to becoming a great quarterback is competitive spirit."[34]
Deliverable (Team Management): Create followership so the team will protect his blindside and follow his direction/audibles without question. **Efforts:** • Able to earn the respect of his teammates through leading by example. • Displays confidence in his abilities and those of the team and coaching staff. Performs with poise and composure. • Accountable, willing to take responsibility for the team's failures, taking pressure off others. • Openly share appreciation and success with other team members.	**Grade: Acceptable +** Brady showed nascent leadership abilities during his two years as a starter at Michigan, carrying the hopes of his teammates, the coaches, and the organization.

<table>
<tr><th>Patriot's Pre-Brady Quarterback Cipher continued</th><th></th></tr>
<tr><td>Deliverable (Company Culture):
Espouse a coachable mindset and be eager to be molded in the Patriot Way. Must have a low ego and trust in the process, following the strategy of the coaching staff without question.
Efforts:
• Able to be coached—listen, take direction, and incorporate that into daily play.
• Display the attitude that nothing is more important than the Patriot franchise and its success.
• Be willing to put the needs of the franchise above his own.</td><td>Grade: Clear Strength

According to Belichick, QB/Assistant coach Dick Rehbein returned from the combine saying that Brady was "the best fit for the [Patriots'] system," with the front office agreeing.*</td></tr>
</table>

Key chapter takeaways

- No one is truly without bias. Make the best decision possible by defining the decision criteria before considering the options, following a process to weigh all options fairly, and acknowledging and adjusting for bias when it creeps into final decision-making.
- Taking steps to remove hidden influences from recruiting and hiring is simply smart business.
- There are nine common biases you should be aware of and actively work to avoid, and a Cipher can help you eliminate bias in your hiring process.

Read it, think it, do it

Reflect on your recent hiring decisions and review the list of biases. Which of them may have played a role in influencing the results?

What did you do to avoid it, or what will you do to make even better decisions in the future?

My commitment: The next time I hire, I will...

CHAPTER TWELVE

Onboarding & Performance Coaching

The hallmark of a well-crafted Cipher is how well it survives the hiring process and lives on as a part of everyday people management. When did you last pull someone's job description to discuss goal setting and performance? Have you ever downloaded the LinkedIn or Indeed posting to onboard your new hire? If the answer is yes, how well did that work?

For most managers, the answer to these questions is typically a chuckle or maybe a sheepish smile. It's a tacit acknowledgment of exactly how ill-suited their job descriptions and postings are when applied to doing the actual work of the job.

Let me ask you a question (and it's a question you probably know the answer to if you've read this far):

Why would you ever use a job description to assess a candidate if you can't use that same document to onboard and coach them?

This chapter will teach you the simple steps to evolve your Cipher from a candidate assessment tool into an evergreen document. This will be the dual-purpose tool that helps new hires come up to speed more quickly and thrive throughout the years they are in this role.

> I recognize that there are terrific resources for developing onboarding plans that go into far more depth than what is covered here. The aim is not to replicate a 200-page onboarding book in this chapter. Rather, I want to ensure that you tie back onboarding efforts to those items you thought were so important to the role of the Cipher.

The Cipher as a critical onboarding tool

Think about the last time you started a new job. What were the top three things you wanted to know? For most people, "what I need to do to be successful" is one of their top answers. The Cipher is the answer to that question and should be the foundation for onboarding a new employee. It covers the essence of the role (Charge), the ultimate measure(s) of success (Outcome), and the most important specifics on how to achieve that success (Deliverables and Efforts).

Timeframe: Prior to their start
Action: Create the onboarding plan

The Cipher makes for an excellent roadmap–but most of the best Ciphers take a multi-year view of the role. This longer view is helpful, but depending on the level of the person you hired, might be overwhelming and/or distracting.

Look through the Cipher and add any specificity needed regarding what the new hire needs to do over the next 6-12 months. Use those goals to set up the immediate needs for onboarding vs. what may be required longer-term.

Related, consider what facts about the organization a new person coming in will need to know, both generically and specifically for this role. This ranges from the mundane (expense reporting, IT help, general policies, and SOPs) to the strategic (new product launches planned, critical threats and opportunities, competitive dynamics).

Depending on your company, you may already have a structured orientation program covering general "get to know the company" information. If not, or if the program needs to be supplemented, make sure you take the time to talk about the mission, vision, and values of the company and/or your specific area within it.

Understanding the values on the wall and the mission statement on the coffee cup is great. Still, it is even better to truly explore the day-to-day values and behaviors that define being a part of your company.

What are the sacred cow issues or other landmines the new hire should know to avoid? Ideally, you've already done a great job of defining this as part of your Culture Deliverable.

Related, who do they need to know?

Who was on your Hiring Board of Advisors, what functions will the new hire support — and get support from—and how will you foster these connections? This includes individuals above them, next to them, and below them in the hierarchy.

The best onboarding plans go beyond simply explaining the functions or even specific names and include a structured set of initial meetings to help make initial connections. You don't need to hold their hand forever, but by making those critical introductions early, you will help them become successful as efficiently as possible.

Where did they excel against the Cipher or fall short?

For this candidate specifically, what developmental areas highlighted on the Cipher will you need to address, and how will you address them? Where did they rate lowest against the Deliverables? Some issues can be resolved through training and development. Consider what coaching you can provide personally, added resources you can bring, or others with whom they can partner.

Given the nature of the gap, how can you help this person grow and change to close that gap? That can include some or all of the following: training courses, developmental sessions, informal conversations with a mentor, an assistant or key lieutenant, a budget for external development, or an executive coach.

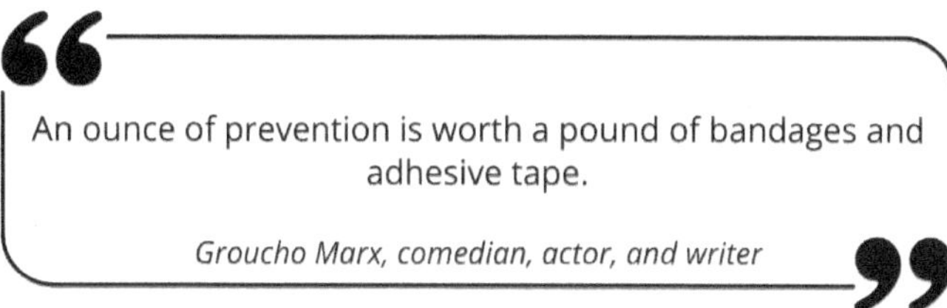

Also, consider what changes you are willing to make to the role. Sometimes, development and training is not enough to close the gap. Especially in unique roles, where there is not a lot of talent available, you may have hired this person knowing that they cannot (or will not) take on a particular Deliverable.

Now is the time to outline how this critical need will be met by others, whether internally or outsourced, etc. In these situations, you should still explain to the new hire that this element *was* a part of the role, and still needs to get done, but that you have solved for it in a different manner. Who knows; perhaps they have an even better solution that they used as a workaround in their prior role.

Invest a bit to make your great new hire even more successful. It's much cheaper and easier than trying to save them if they struggle!

Timeframe: First month of employment
Action: Onboard with the Cipher

Let's assume you have created an onboarding plan based on the Cipher and our advice above. Now, convey all of this valuable information on Day One, using the Cipher to kick off the onboarding discussion. It will be the tool that you and your new hire, as well as other key stakeholders, can use to create and maintain alignment on what matters most!

It is critical to have this conversation from a developmental standpoint. I never show the exact ratings and commentary when sharing the Cipher with a new hire because when our brains are tuned into being assessors, everyone can write some pretty blunt content.

And that's fine—that's the role of an assessor. But remember as you move towards onboarding, you are now this person's developer/coach and need to focus on how to help them grow, not to take their legs out from under them completely. No one wants to start their new job learning how they weren't really a fit, but were the least-awful option!

If the new employee is a leader or manager, use the Cipher to cascade goals and responsibilities with their team.

This will be fairly easy to do if Ciphers have been well-adopted within your organization. The new leader will have a Cipher alignment conversation with their new team; they will share their individual Ciphers, and it will be clear how the pieces of their team all dovetail with each other.

If your company is not there yet, you will need help to facilitate this process. Consider a series of one-to-one meetings between the new leader and each of their direct reports where the new leader shares their own Cipher and a highlighted/marked-up version of where they believe this person should be contributing.

At the same time, the new leader should leave enough room for the direct report to name the areas they think they should focus on. The key is to get clarity on how things truly work within the organization while also giving the leader clarity on who will handle what *and* assuring that all team members share that clarity.

Timeframe: Month two and beyond
Action: Ongoing performance coaching

Let's start with the basic premise: it is far easier to provide performance coaching when the individual knows what is expected of them, and, before performance has become a big issue. Make performance coaching and feedback an ongoing element of how you manage your team and watch how well they grow!

As a performance coaching tool, the Cipher is excellent off-the-shelf because it enables a conversation about where the person is today, what they are naturally good at, and where they have room to develop. Therefore, the Cipher is the basis for two critical conversations: the quarterly or bimonthly check-in and the annual development mentoring/coaching discussion.

Quarterly or bimonthly check-ins

Use the adjusted/annualized goals version of the Cipher to fuel a one-to-one conversation with your new employee on a regular basis.

The goal is a substantive but light conversation about how things are going, where they think they are trending (at or above the success line), and where they might need help. The first part of the conversation, even at the organization's highest ranks, should celebrate that person's successes.

This is not only to give them the proverbial pat on the back, but also to reinforce those behaviors they need to continue doing. After all, if failure is the best teacher, then success is not; so, make sure they know what they are doing that makes a difference.

At the same time, make sure you also focus on those things that may be putting their success at risk. What actions do the two of you need to take today that will get the Deliverables back on track by the end of the year? What behavior, if left unchecked, could derail them? Or even what haven't they gotten to yet, and now that they've been in the role a while, your expectations are increasing and they need to address it.

Finally, don't forget about development!

As you talk through actions and decisions, remember the compromise and commitment you made when you hired them. No one is a perfect fit for any Cipher, so ensure you have done what you promised to support their growth.

Annual performance and goal-setting conversation

Once a year, take a step back and examine the larger picture. How well have they performed against their annual goals? How does that compare to the original multi-year Cipher you first created?

The goal of this discussion is to add-in those elements they haven't tackled yet and otherwise reset on performance expectations for the following year. This can also be a good time to reset the longer-term Cipher vision for the role.

Why update it?

If your organization is rapidly growing and thriving, or if the person has developed themselves, then last year's Cipher may no longer be relevant! Perhaps they have made massive headway on many items and driven their performance far beyond what you thought it would be 12 months ago. The new hire's scope and responsibilities may have expanded, and the nature of what they need to do to achieve those goals has changed. The other benefit is that should you need to expand the department and hire more people, 95% of the Cipher work is already done!

Craig's real-world story

An Aesop Partners client hired a new CEO, who was assessed using a Cipher developed with the internal team and board. We then partnered with the board and the new CEO to co-create an onboarding plan that addressed the business's needs and the CEO's specific development needs from the Cipher document. The process was launched... and then the Covid-19 pandemic hit.

Our work collectively through the Cipher process meant the CEO was ready to take immediate action before the pandemic forced a shutdown. He was far better integrated into the company as well.

He and his team worked through the inevitable hurdles of coming together while leading a regionalized organization virtually, and the business thrived. The Cipher-driven approach enabled a laser-like focus on the CEO's most critical development areas vs. a more generic "get to know this place and come up with a plan" approach that would have substantially hindered the company given the global pandemic.

Aesop's modern fable

Patagonia's CHRO Dean Carter and CEO Rose Marcario started a revolution in 2015. The company's top leadership recognized they needed a more relevant, impactful, and agile approach to goal setting and performance management. They wanted a mechanism to showcase who they were as a company and the values most important to their employees.

They uncovered that performance management appeared to be an area that took a lot of time, energy, and effort without many tangible benefits. They shifted from a traditional annual review to a "regenerative approach" that utilizes continuous and scheduled feedback.

With this new method, ongoing feedback populates a database of performance-related information, which is then used for annual reviews and quarterly conversations. Carter believes it's what happens in between those yearly meetings that truly drives better employee performance. Getting real-time feedback has allowed their associates to identify strengths and weaknesses more closely, resulting in immediate course-correcting rather than waiting for an annual review.

In a recent survey, 70% of the retailer's employees stated they had received feedback the week prior and consequently changed their behavior.[36] Patagonia employees believe reviewing goals regularly, like the Deliverables established within the Cipher, is the best feedback form.

In 2018, the company reported that employees who received higher bonuses were more likely to have requested feedback and completed a check-in, as well as their annual review. That correlates to their statement in 2020 that their employee turnover rate dipped to an impressive 4%.

Key chapter takeaways

- Use the Cipher as the springboard when developing your onboarding plan.
- Support your new hire with the development (or other adjustments) they need to overcome the Cipher gaps identified during the interview process.
- Transform a Cipher from an assessment tool into a performance coaching guide to maximize impact.

Read it, think it, do it

Think about your organization's approach to onboarding today.

Which of your last hires would have benefited most by taking a Cipher-driven approach to onboarding?

What might they have done differently if you used the Cipher to drive alignment from the start?

What might the broader implications have been for your team and company?

« PART V: Ciphers Unleashed »

The sky is not the limit, it's just the beginning.

Chuck Yeager, United States Air Force officer, flying ace, and record-setting test pilot

Chapter Thirteen

Cipher Application Beyond the Office

As I was writing this book and developing the concept of a Cipher, I had an *Aha!* moment related to some excellent mentorship I received. I had a treasured mentor who had passed away in late 2018. When I last asked him for his thoughts on which career opportunities I should or should not take, he chuckled but refused to help me, saying "That's the wrong question Craig."

Alan changed my perspective from thinking about the next move to thinking about the end-game. Figuring out what job I should take next wasn't important...yet.

Instead, he helped me see that I needed to ask myself, "What do I want my life to look like in 20 years? Who is Craig at 60? What have I accomplished, who am I as a husband, father, friend, and business leader?"

> The secret of change is to focus all of your energy not on fighting the old, but on building the new.
>
> *Socrates, ancient Greek philosopher*

Once I understood the end goal, he gave me another query: "What strengths and attributes, successes and failures, and experiences will I need to enable myself to get to that point?" We discussed what I was good at already, what needed to be added to my toolkit, and how I could close those gaps. That clarity made my next move crystal clear, because it was all about improving my self-rating against my own personal Cipher!

The Cipher process can apply to any big decision

You can create a Cipher for just about anything! After all, at the heart of the Cipher are four simple elements: a quick overview statement defining the end goal, a definitive way to measure success, a breakdown of the pieces required to create that success, and enough definition of those pieces to make it happen. It's not such a difficult *CODE* to figure out.

When you view it that way, what types of decisions can use an approach like this? Frankly, there are few big decisions that would *not* benefit from a process like this.

What are the job-like situations where a Job Cipher approach would be beneficial?

- Evaluating board members or officers for an organization/nonprofit.
- Choosing players for your sports teams (IRL or fantasy leagues).
- Selecting students for internships, scholarships, or even admissions.
- Evaluating members for highly selective civic or fraternal groups.

What are other types of decisions where a Cipher can help you make better choices?

- In what career can I find the most success?
- What college is right for me?
- How can I find greater spiritual fulfillment?
- What type of volunteer opportunities should I pursue?
- What hobbies or activities could further enrich my life?

Some of you may need more clarification about the broader use of our approach. So, I sat down and quickly created the Marriage Cipher shown below. Don't worry, I told my wife that we rated a Clear Strength against all elements!

Craig's Marriage Cipher 
Charge: A challenging and vital partner to build a lifetime of happiness and fulfillment for an ambitious young person.
Outcome: To happily celebrate our 50th wedding anniversary with no regrets about the person we chose.
Deliverable: Create, raise, and love two to three children. **Efforts**: • Desire a family of that size. • Be willing to sacrifice as needed for the children. • Always take a team-based approach, regardless of a man-on-man or zone defense. • Share my fundamental values about how our children should be raised.
Deliverable: Put up with, or even fully engage in, a humorous and irreverent yet value-driven team culture. **Efforts**: • Accept me for who I am and love me for it. • Call me out when appropriate but in a loving manner that doesn't make me feel "wrong." • Truly love people and see the delight, wonder, and possibility in humanity. • Share or respect my spiritual beliefs and core values.
Deliverable: Set a clear vision for the future and measure daily hiccups with a long-term view. **Efforts**: • Share my intention for one marriage that lasts the entirety of our lives. • Regularly engage in forward-thinking, setting intentions and goals towards the life we want to create. • Live with a long-term perspective; recognize that nothing is perfect and accept the tablespoons of "bad" along with the pints of "good." • Recognize that forgiveness is a gift we give ourselves and expect to give that gift often for my failings!

Craig's Marriage Cipher continued

Deliverable: Contribute as an equal partner to the tangible aspects of running the household and building a life.

Efforts:

- Before kids, work with me to provide the financial resources for living while saving for the future.
- Share equally in household chores, respecting that we may each be better at specific tasks.
- Care for me when I am sick and accept care when you are.
- As parents, share equally in the care of our children.

Deliverable: Actively grow according to shared values, providing and accepting challenges from your partner.

Efforts:

- Understand your values with clarity.
- Related, be honest with yourself and me regarding what truly matters to you.
- Take stock of yourself, me, and us occasionally, and suggest improvements to strengthen our marriage and family for the long term.
- Genuinely desire to become an even better person throughout your life.

Deliverable: Be the person who makes me irrationally and irreversibly in love with you.

Efforts:

- Be attractive to me.
- Love yourself and give love to others.
- Be caring and kind.
- Love dogs and boats.

A combination of the mind and heart

The wonderful thing about using a Cipher to evaluate your spouse is its applicability for regular performance coaching. *I'm kidding, darling!*

Applying the Cipher process to marriage started out as a joke with my writing collaborators. But then we did it. And it struck us as an incredibly unexpected and excellent example of how you can bring decision clarity to what many would consider being all about "the soft stuff."

How many fewer divorces would there be if people paused and checked their gut instinct with a Cipher before taking the plunge? Readers married in the Catholic church or similar religions may recall their Pre-Cana classes, which were *Cipher creation discussions!*

In fact, a recent study found that in states that enforced pre-marital counseling requirements, "divorce rates were about 0.5 to 1.5 percent lower than states with no such requirements. The study's author noted that the statistics could be underestimating the programs' effectiveness."[37]

Maybe we stumbled onto something...but I digress. Whether you use the Cipher to determine your life partner or not, I hope you take away the insight of the greater benefits of the Cipher process. Not only will you become a better interviewer and possibly a better manager, but you may also see the benefit in other major decisions in your life. It offers a way to bring hard science and analysis to even the most soft and emotional aspects of life.

The Cipher marries (some pun intended) these two approaches, bringing the art and science of decision-making together to help you achieve success.

Applying the Cipher framework to personal decisions requires being thoughtful about your definition of success and how you'll get there. This is the science.

At the same time, evaluating Cipher Deliverables for many of these questions requires much more finesse than when creating a Job Cipher. This is the art.

I passionately believe that many more people would be happier in their work and personal lives if they took the time to break down big decisions into several little ones.

That's precisely what I desire for you: happiness and success. Happiness in the people you hire, the job you choose, and even the partner you decide to spend your life with.

Key chapter takeaways

- Decision-making is hard, and making good decisions is even harder, especially when you try to tackle the whole question all at once. How do you eat an elephant? One bite at a time. The same is true with decision-making. Make that scary big decision far easier by tackling the five to seven smaller decisions that will show you the best path.

- Try applying this process to your next big decision and see how you can achieve clarity with a balance of art and science.

Read it, think it, do it

Is there a big decision you have to make in your life? Try making a Cipher.

- Describe what you ultimately want in one colorful and impactful sentence: that's the Charge.
- How will you measure success, or know when you've achieved that objective? That is your Outcome.
- How will you achieve that success? Those are your Deliverables, and I'm sure you know the rest.

Once you have it built, share it with a friend or trusted advisor. Reflect on how that helps you choose the right path forward.

Chapter Fourteen

Next Steps & Final Thoughts

We have come to the end of our time together, and I hope you will take the time to acknowledge all that you have done. We've covered a lot of ground together!

To recap what you've learned:

- In Part I, you studied why the typical approach to hiring doesn't work, and that there are clear benefits to using a Cipher-driven approach.
- In Part II, you explored the specifics of building a thoughtful and thorough Cipher. With the CODE acronym, you can create the building blocks for success in your next hiring challenge.
- Part III taught you how to take your Cipher to the next level. You learned how to bring in key stakeholders and make the document even more robust.
- In Part IV, you learned how to put the Cipher to use. The importance of structured interviews and how to

grade your Cipher was discussed. Using the Cipher for onboarding as well as how to apply it for ongoing performance management was also explored.

- Finally, in Part V, you saw how you can take your Cipher learnings and apply them just about anywhere. It's not just about hiring and team management.

The next step is simple: put your learning into action!

At the beginning of our journey, I shared that people who struggle to get the right employees into the right roles either don't know what to do or aren't doing what they know they should be doing.

You now know exactly what to do.

I hope you love this approach as much as I do, and get even more benefit than I have promised you! Better still, I hope you share the knowledge you have learned with others, because everyone deserves a chance to make the best decisions, hiring or otherwise.

The Cipher mindset is thought-provoking, challenging, sometimes scary, often exciting, but always powerful. I have never seen a hiring situation made *worse* by the creation of a Cipher, and almost always made it remarkably better.

The cost of money and time wasted undoing a hiring mistake or living with a bad hire is exponentially worse than the hour or two you'll spend to create a Cipher for your most important decisions.

Remember the underlying philosophy of the Cipher: If you can't define the destination, the journey to get there is impossible.

To that end, at HireBest.ai, you can continue getting support and advice about all the concepts in this book. Use the resources mentioned in the book, join one of our highly acclaimed learning programs, or even use our HireBest platform to bring an AI-enabled structured hiring approach directly to your organization easily.

I am truly honored that you have taken the time out of your busy schedule to read this book and learn the Cipher way.

I hope these principles, strategies, and techniques positively impact your ability to build exceptional teams and make phenomenal decisions!

Endnotes

1. Murphy, Mark. "Why New Hires Fail." Leadership IQ, 2011, https://www.leadershipiq.com/blogs/leadershipiq/35354241-why-new-hires-fail-emotional-intelligence-vs-skills

2. Smart, Geoff, and Randy Street. Who: A Method for Hiring. Ballantine Books, 2008.

3. M.P. McEnrue, Perceived competence as a moderator of the relationship between role clarity and job performance: A test of two hypotheses, Organizational Behavior and Human Performance, Volume 34, Issue 3, Dec. 1984, https://doi.org/10.1016/0030-5073(84)90044-8

4. Levashina, J., Hartwell, C. J., Morgeson, F. P., & Campion, M. A. (2014). The structured employment interview: Narrative and quantitative review of the research literature. Personnel Psychology, 67(1), 241–293, https://doi.org/10.1111/peps.12052

5. Economy, Peter. "11 Interesting Hiring Statistics You Should Know." Inc., 5 May 2015, https://www.inc.com/peter-economy/19-interesting-hiring-statistics-you-should-know.html

6. Partners, ICIMS. "Best Practices Rolling Out iCIMS to Your Hiring Managers."2020, https://community.icims.com/resource/15204392 24000 /BestPracticesHMRollingOut#:~:text=Page%207,they%20recruit%2C%20but%2061%25%20of

7. Deutsch, Matt. "Why Candidates Are Turning Down a Job Offer from Your Client." Top Echelon, 15 May 2020, https://www.topechelon.com/blog/placement-process/why-candidates-are-turning-down-a-job-offer-from-your-client/

8. Staff. "Top Recruitment Statistics for 2019 - Workonic." Workonic Limited, 3 May 2019, http://www.workonic.com/top-recruitment-statistics-of-2019/

9. Staff, North America. "Should Hiring Be Based on Gut – or Data?" Knowledge@Wharton, 24 Aug. 2015, https://knowledge.wharton.upenn.edu/article/should-hiring-be-based-on-gut-or-data/

10. Götting, Marie Charlotte. "Best-Selling Artists of All Time Worldwide." Statista, 25 September 2025, https://www.statista.com/statistics/271174/top-selling-artists-in-the-united-states/. Accessed 25 Sept. 2025.

11. Best-Selling Artists of All Time (Daily Update) - Chartmasters, https://chartmasters.org/best-selling-artists-of-all-time/.Accessed 25 Sept. 2025.

12. Published by Patrick Leu, "Highest Grossing Concert Tours Worldwide 2024." Statista, 15 Jan. 2025, http://www.statista.com/statistics/278378/the-most-successful-music-tours-worldwide/.Accessed 25 Sept. 2025.

13. Lewis, Michael. Moneyball: The Art of Winning an Unfair Game. W.W. Norton, 2013.

14. "Mars Probe Lost Due to Simple Math Error." Los Angeles Times, 1 Oct. 1999, https://www.latimes.com/archives/la-xpm-1999-oct-01-mn-17288-story.html

15. Prokesch, Steven. "Can Don Burr Go Back to the Future?" The New York Times, 6 July 1986, https://www.nytimes.com/1986/07/06/business/people-express-a-case-study-can-don-burr-go-back-to-the-future.html

16. Boudette, Neal E. "Elon Musk Predicts Tesla Driverless Taxi Fleet Next Year." The New York Times, 22 Apr. 2019, https://www.nytimes.com/2019/04/22/business/elon-musk-tesla-autopilot.html

17. Clifford, Catherine. "Elon Musk: 'I Need to Figure out How to Be Better....and Then We Can Be Better at Meeting Goals'." CNBC, April 13, 2018, https://www.cnbc.com/2018/04/13/elon-musk-talks-to-gayle-king-about-meeting-tesla-goals.html

18. "Executive, Author Robert Townsend Dies." The Washington Post, 14 Jan. 1998, https://www.washington post.com/archive/local/1998/01/14/executive-author-robert-townsend-dies/ced04fd9-2a0c-4b82-b277-e7f372f7d4aa/

19. Engelmeier, Sheila. "Did Mary Barra's Inclusive Leadership Style Propel Her to The Top?" Industry Week, 22 Jan. 2014, https://www.industryweek.com/leadership/companies-executives/article/21962100/did-mary-barras-inclusive-leadership-style-propel-her-to-the-top/

20. Vlasic, Bill. "New G.M. Chief Is Company Woman, Born to It." The New York Times, 10 Dec. 2013, https://www.nytimes.com/2013/12/11/business/gm-names-first-female-chief-executive.html

21. La Monica, Paul R. "Target's Brian Cornell Is the Top CEO of 2019." CNN, Cable News Network, 18 Dec. 2019, https://www.cnn.com/2019/12/18/investing/target-brian-cornell-ceo-of-the-year/

22. Hunt, Dame Vivian, et al. "Delivering through Diversity." McKinsey & Company, 17 Jan. 2020, https://www.mckinsey.com/business-functions/organization/our-insights/delivering-through-diversity/

23. Agarwal, Dr. Pragya. "Here Is How Bias Can Affect Recruitment in Your Organisation." Forbes, Forbes Magazine, 19 Oct. 2018, https://www.forbes.com/sites/pragyaagarwaleurope/2018/10/19/how-can-bias-during-interviews-affect-recruitment-in-your-organisation/?sh=2599a7ca1951/

24. Herring, Cedric. "Does Diversity Pay? Race, Gender, and the Business Case for Diversity." American Sociological Review, Vol. 74, No. 2, Apr. 2009, https://www.jstor.org/stable/27736058

25. Bush, Matt. "Why Is Diversity & Inclusion in the Workplace Important?" Great Place to Work®, 2021, https://greatplacetowork.com.au/blog/why-is-diversity-inclusion-in-the-workplace-important/

26. Knight, Rebecca. "7 Practical Ways to Reduce Bias in Your Hiring Process." SHRM, 16 Aug. 2019, https://www.shrm.org/topics-tools/news/talent-acquisition/7-practical-ways-to-reduce-bias-hiring-process

27. Malhotra, Ruchika T. "How to Reduce Personal Bias When Hiring." Harvard Business Review, 16 July 2020, https://hbr.org/2019/06/how-to-reduce-personal-bias-when-hiring

28. Benson, Buster. "Cognitive bias cheat sheet, simplified." Medium, 8 Jan. 2017, https://medium.com/thinking-is-hard/4-conundrums-of-intelligence-2ab78d90740f

29. Echevarria, Desiree. "9 Hiring Biases Hurting Your Recruiting Efforts - How to Avoid Common Interview Bias." CareerPlug, 9 June 2021, https://www.careerplug.com/9-hiring-biases-that-are-hurting-your-recruiting-efforts/

30. Johnson, Alexandra. "13 Common Hiring Biases to Watch Out For." Harver, 14 May 2021, https://harver.com/blog/hiring-biases

31. Warje, Kira. "Action Bias." The Decision Lab, 22 Jan. 2021, https://thedecisionlab.com/biases/action-bias

32. Musa, Hanen. "How Tom Brady Became Lowest NFL Draft Pick to Have the Most Touchdowns." Sports News, Sportskeeda, 08 Nov. 2022, https://www.sportskeeda.com/nfl/how-tom-brady-became-lowest-nfl-draft-pick-touchdowns

33. Reiss, Mike. "Tom Brady's 'Favorite' NFL Combine Picture Celebrates 20th Birthday." ESPN, 26 Feb. 2020, https://www.espn.com/blog/new-england-patriots/post/_/id/4819386/tom-bradys-favorite-nfl-combine-picture-celebrates-20th-birthday

34. Dodd, Brian. "Urban Meyer's 5 Qualities of a Great Quarterback." Brian Dodd on Leadership, 16 Oct 2019, https://briandoddonleadership.com/2019/10/15/urban-meyers-5-qualities-of-a-great-quarterback/

35. Gaines, Cork. "Tom Brady Was the Biggest Steal in NFL Draft History, but There Was More to It Than Just Luck." Business Insider, 3 Feb. 2019, https://www.businessinsider.com/patriots-draft-tom-brady-2017-1

36. Cook Ramirez, Julie. "The Future of Feedback." HRExecutive.com, 26 Apr. 2018, https://hrexecutive.com/future-of-feedback/

37. Rousselle, Christine. "Study Shows Marriage Prep Can Drive down Divorce." Catholic News Agency, 20 Mar 2024, http://ewtnnews.com/world/us/study-shows-marriage-prep-can-drive-down-divorce?redirectedfrom=cna

www.ingramcontent.com/pod-product-compliance
Lightning Source LLC
LaVergne TN
LVHW090514110826
845146LV00003B/847

* 9 7 9 8 2 3 4 0 3 8 2 3 4 *